PHENOMENOLOGICAL PHILOSOPHY

And Reconstruction In Western Theism

Allan M. Savage

WESTBOW
P R E S S

WestBow Press books may be ordered through booksellers or by contacting:

WestBow Press
A Division of Thomas Nelson
1663 Liberty Drive
Bloomington, IN 47403
www.westbowpress.com
1-(866) 928-1240

Because of the dynamic nature of the Internet, any Web addresses or links contained in this book may have changed since publication and may no longer be valid. The views expressed in this work are solely those of the author and do not necessarily reflect the views of the publisher, and the publisher hereby disclaims any responsibility for them.

ISBN: 978-1-4497-0265-6 (sc)
ISBN: 978-1-4497-0266-3 (e)

Library of Congress Control Number: 2010928776

Printed in the United States of America

WestBow Press rev. date: 6/16/2010

In memory of
Leslie Sutherland Dewart 1922 – 2009

Contents

Foreword

Twenty-five years ago I had the good fortune to meet and work with Fr Allan Savage in the RENEW program conducted within the Roman Catholic Diocese of Thunder Bay. While Fr Savage became the Director of the program for the Diocese, I undertook responsibility in one parish. Under his leadership, the RENEW program proved exceptionally successful throughout the Diocese. I experienced personal fulfilment through my participation in this achievement owing in great measure to Fr Savage's knowledge and his dedication to the task. His inspiration and selfless contribution ensured an auspicious conclusion to the program.

Since those early years of RENEW, I have studied under his guidance in the pursuit of a Master's degree in Theology, always cognizant of his rare gifts as teacher, mentor, pastor and friend. His depth of knowledge, love of learning, and capability with the written word, has led him, after authoring several books, to this one for which I feel honoured to have been asked to write the Foreword.

It is with his same sense of dedication that Fr Savage has contributed, through this book, to the extant body of philosophical and theological work. In this very personal account he has expressed his evolutionary thinking from dependency on a traditional Thomistic theological view based on classical Hellenist philosophy to a phenomenological methodology. It is this innovative view, which has captured the imagination of the more enlightened and daring of contemporary theologians and philosophers.

The approach Fr Savage takes reflects the probable if not inevitable metamorphosis from a classical to a contemporary view of theology. The book is an excellent teaching tool, one, which faithfully reflects the word of God. He stresses that through personal engagement with the Spirit of God one may begin to understand religious experience, thereby enabling one's personal faith conviction. In this regard, Fr Savage explains that the primary purpose of theological study is spiritual growth, while intellectual understanding is of secondary importance.

The deepening of theological understanding, the author explains, has been achieved, not by ecclesiastical officials, but by faithful individuals sometimes even in opposition to official interpretation. Thus, he sees the necessity of official recognition of the *sensus fidelium*, which must be recognize as an essential element in the development of doctrine. Institutional and traditional edicts are no longer viable if given unilaterally from on high. Furthermore, the author says, individuals need to accept their co-responsibility and co-creative relationships with that which is divine. A viable future Church, he says, must relinquish its hold on sovereignty and centralization and institute a decision-making procedure through the principle of subsidiarity.

Fr Savage reaches beyond contemporary understanding of Christianity in order to embrace a fresh, intellectual approach. He explains that the Roman Catholic Church is on the verge of supplanting Thomistic philosophy by abandoning traditional theoretical understanding. His incursion into the constructs of the Modernist movement clarifies new interpretations within theological thinking illuminating the potential for development in the future Church. Theologians have perceived the classical understanding of truth incorrectly and as valid as the truth itself. Such interpretation, he insists, is an aberration. He sees a natural and necessary evolution in thinking from a fixed idea to a relational and dynamic conception of truth.

The ideas expressed by Fr Savage in his book raise theological, problematical questions for the traditional reader, but serve as a major source of theological exploration. Humanity must have, he says, the freedom to discuss theological mystery through experiential philosophy as opposed to the traditional, rigid Thomistic philosophy. Fundamentalism presents what he refers as an irresolvable problem with respect to the development of Christian theism.

As the Diocese prepares to revisit a RENEW program, the concepts discussed in Fr Savage's book become remarkably provocative and timely. He has envisioned a Church, which has achieved a renewal, a metamorphic movement from Thomistic philosophy to phenomenological theology. Compelling in its persuasive recording of a life, which has experienced a significant renewal, the book presents a rethinking in the mind of Fr Savage of traditional Church theology. Sometimes challenging, always intriguing, and never lacking a depth of perception, this chronicle presents a text, which shows how the author has undergone a deeply inspiring reinterpretation of theological concepts.

This book passes as not only an informative guide to reflection on interpretation of truth but serves as a must-read for any serious student of theology. It has been personally satisfying for me to read the text and to respond to the ramifications of a journey of faith, which compels the reader to examine his or her own life in the search for truth. I heartily recommend this book not only for the student of theology but for all who wish to gain insights into the potential for a renewed Church, a dynamic and living theology, and personal growth.

James J. Bishop
Thunder Bay, Ontario
March 2010

SECTION ONE

1 INTRODUCTION

This book arises from a personal reflection. It is a suggested reconstruction of Christian theism [1] arising out of phenomenological philosophy, which appears to be gaining acceptance in Catholic theological circles since Vatican II. Henri Bergson (1859 – 1941) has influenced my thinking in this regard. He observes that philosophy is the study of becoming in general and, as a continuation of science, is not a certain new scholasticism that has grown up during the latter half of the nineteenth century around the physics of Galileo, as the old scholasticism grew up around Aristotle. This monograph is an account of my thinking as it has been affected by my experience over the years of my pastoral and academic career. Although this monograph arises within a particular Catholic theological perspective the ideas and notions discussed, I believe, have significance for an ecumenical Christian theology. This book is based on a phenomenological philosophical reflection, as opposed to a presentation of an uncritical exposé of ideas. That is to say, the ideas I present here have been reflected upon, considered and re-considered. Also, not just my initial insights, but additional insights arising from my reflections, have been reflected upon, considered and re-considered before I presented them here.

I present my thoughts by selecting certain notions that have caught my attention within Christian theistic theology. Such selecting is proper to the phenomenological philosophical stance according to Johan van

---

1 By theism I mean contemporary theistic theology. I use this term for convenience sake, even though it derives from a traditional philosophical point of view, which I no longer favour.

Rensburg (2007) who notes that qualitative research works on a much smaller scale than quantitative research. Following the thinking of Philip Hughes, I preserve the distinction between theistic theology, or theism, which addresses the issues that arise within the context of faith and require individual attention and, religious studies, which address the ideas that arise within the context of religion and are just what the words indicate – the study of religion. Hughes (1947) describes theologians as thinkers who face the task of explaining the traditional doctrine in a systematic manner, using natural knowledge and its laws to make the divinely revealed truth more intelligible, thus distinguishing them from students of religion. The critical reader will recognize this distinction between theology and religious studies and value further the conscious insights that arise from an understanding of theism in contrast to the theoretical knowledge gained from a religious understanding. The former, theism, or critical theology, which is dependent on philosophy assists in the spiritual maturation of the individual. Whereas the latter, religious studies, is dependent primarily on sociology and assists in the intellectual maturation of the individual. Given this distinction, then, I examine the on-going spiritual maturation of the individual and his or her responsibility for the Word of God, or the reconstruction of Western theism.

II THEISTIC THEOLOGY AS RESPONSIBILITY FOR THE WORD OF GOD

Theologians have a responsibility for the Word of God, which has been revealed to their communities of faith; be they Jewish, Christian or Muslim.   I also suggest that theologians of these particular communities of faith have a responsibility to each other. As well, they have a responsibility to others who are outside their particular faith communities and who are seeking an understanding of the experience of God. I include among them those who adhere to communities that present alternative concepts of the Deity. In other words, theologians have a responsibility to the contemporary pluralistic society, that is, to the public square; be it a religious or a secular public square. Following Yuval Lurie (2000) I suggest that theological responsibility arises within the cultural order, not the natural order, since it requires a social context for it to come into existence and a certain philosophical character to affect human beings. While human nature is everywhere recognized as being the same, human cultures change from place to place. Further, by secular I mean a public square that embraces the philosophical systems and cultures that profess no revelation as understood in Jewish, Christian or Muslim traditions. An argument could be made, I suppose, that theologians have, as well, a responsibility to atheistic cultures, which differ from secular cultures. However, I exclude any argument for that responsibility from my consideration. I consider atheistic cultures, rather, as more properly data for a sociological study, not a theological study.

It is required of theologians that they exercise critical philosophical reflective thinking, but such thinking is not required by all who are religiously inclined and who may be satisfied with the explanations offered by myth and folklore (Kolbe, 1944). Traditionally, critical philosophical thinking is carried on within, not without, a community of faith which has experienced divine revelation. It is the community of faith that mediates the experiences of the believer and acts as the agent to pass on to future generations the insights of the community's theological reflections on divine revelation. Thus, the theologian cannot be separated from the faith community in his or her philosophical reflection. Therefore, it almost goes without saying that in theological reflection critical collaboration, within the community, is necessary among scholars of many disciplines. By critical collaboration I do not mean a critical evaluation according to contemporary political, cultural and philosophical conventions whose standards tend to exclude personal preferences for the sake of common principles. Rather, I mean a conscious critical examination, which transcends those standards of political, cultural and philosophical conventions and allows for personal preference, without forsaking common principles. That is, I understand critical collaboration to involve a clear, consistent, professional, systematic and conscious sharing of philosophical insights into the personal, but not private, experience of God. Such understanding constitutes the reflective theological character of this book.

Philosophy, among all the disciplines available to assist the theologian in this task of critical collaboration, is the most fundamental and appropriate. Philosophy is an intellectual and acquired way of evaluating experience. That is, philosophy is opposed to folklore or myth as a way of interpreting experience. For the interested student, a valuable introductory study to this distinction is to be found in Harry Girvetz, George Geiger, Harold Hantz and Bertam Morris (1966), *Science,*

Folklore and Philosophy. Today, in particular, existential philosophical questions, not the idealist questions of yesteryear, attract the attention of many religious thinkers. However, in this existential attraction, no one can formulate all the right questions much less all the right answers. An appeal is frequently made today by theologians to an existential philosophical way of thinking to account for the experience of the faithful of various religious communities. There is no denying that, in many instances, an existential way of thinking is currently replacing the classical way of thinking in interpreting religious experience. Not religious studies, as is often popularly and erroneously assumed, but an existential philosophy of life is the proper *locus* for theological inquiry in the contemporary context. In this inquiry, then, I posit that an existential theology discloses the intentional contents of the human mind.

An existential theistic theology is not restricted to denominational ecclesial communities, nor synagogues and mosques. In transcending denominational interests an existential theism is less likely to become inordinately influenced by any institutional and political ideology, thus being free to responsibly address the Word of God. An existential theism concerns the individual person in community, not the person in isolation. Thus, in an existential theism particular institutional and political concerns are secondary in interpreting one's experience. It is worth noting Yuval Lurie's (2000) distinction between an explanation and an interpretation. Explanations are called for in connection with what is not understood outright. Interpretations are called for in connection with what is understood but to which we want further insight. Should theological theistic theology fail at transcending institutional interests and become a mere servant of a community's societal experience this would be tantamount to failing in its responsibility for the Word of God. Sometimes it appears that critical thinking in theism does not rise above a societal understanding. It might appear that critical thinking sometimes degenerates to being satisfied with the popular place allotted to it by civil and secular intellectuals in Western culture. The point I want to emphasize is that we ought to be aware of the danger of a loss of identity and purpose, when theologizing, in this age of mass communication where the rhetoric is becoming more important than the religion. The uncritical rhetoric of contemporary culture, which supports agnosticism, immanentism, epistemological and moral relativism, as well as theoretical and practical materialism, renders theism no longer a sacred science. Not being a sacred science, then, theism fails in its responsibility for the Word of God.

As noted, all theism, existential and speculative, must be distinguished from religious studies, which is a separate discipline in its own right. As a separate and distinct academic discipline religious studies is rooted in the Western academic way of thinking of the mid to late 19th Century. In its pedigree religious studies lists such diverse disciplines as linguistics, historiography, anthropology, ethnology, archaeology, and sociology. In contemporary academic thinking religious studies extends beyond the Western Christian religious traditions and seeks to inquire into the religious expression of other cultures besides that of the West. Thus, Oriental and Asian cultural expressions of belief are also of interest to religious studies. Theistic theology also has changed and has developed as a contemporary academic way of thinking leaving its Mediaeval foundations for a modern intellectual understanding arising out of the experience of the Enlightenment and Reformation. However, theistic theology as far as most professionals are concerned, is still perceived to be exclusively at the service of persons preparing to minister in the interests of a particular revealed religious tradition. To the contrary, I suggest that in the contemporary Western cultural context an existential theism recognises that its primary purpose is as a *ministerium verbi divini* (service to the Word of God) and thus has a responsibility for the Word of God, not only for particular religious traditions.

Christian existential theism is nothing less than a personal encounter with the Spirit of God in interpreting religious experience. It expresses the believer's confession and conviction which arises from this personal encounter. Thus, theologians cannot conceive theism merely as an academic subject. As merely an academic subject, theism would reveal particular convictional norms, or the lack of such norms. To my mind, merely addressing the convictional norms of the believer as an academic subject is more properly the domain of religious studies. Further, the disciplines that make up the *loci* for theological reflection today are not necessarily the ones that have been accepted by the academics of classical philosophy when reflecting on God's activity in the believer's life. Theologians must direct their interest primarily to the revelation of God, as given in scripture and ecclesial tradition. Secondarily, dialogue, with contemporary artists, musicians, novelists, poets and philosophers present contemporary *loci* for theological reflection. Although scripture, not a convictional norm is the primary *locus* for theology, a convictional norm is an important secondary *locus* for philosophical reflection.

The old metaphysical quests for a God that can be rationally proved are futile in the contemporary world. Further, any mystical quest for a religious experience tells us nothing of God's nature. Thus, the contemporary existential theologian does not look for a polemic opportunity to prove a point about God's existence. Rather, expressing and clarifying the experience of faith, lived historically, is the existential theologian's primary concern. Within this experience of faith there are certain *existentialia*, which contextualize the believer's experience, which the contemporary existential theologian must take into consideration. These *existentialia* are fear, despair, love, hope, suffering, death, happiness, finiteness and guilt. But, these *existentialia* constitute only half of the theological equation, the human part (*a partis hominis*), not God's part (*a parte Dei*). For Christians the *logos* was incarnated into these *existentialia*. For the existential theologian, it is self-evident that serious questions arise on both parts. My Christian life may be legally private but it is, at the same time, morally public in the modern Western world. Thus, my Christian duty, that is to say, my Christian response cannot merely be a reaction to the social and political forms of life. My Christian response arises from more than that. My Christian response is constitutive of my life such that it relates me to the larger community. Through this relationship to the larger community, theological developments, which ultimately bring about transformation in the community, originate within my experience. Conversely, theological developments, which bring about a transformation in me, originate within the community.

As a result of Vatican II Roman Catholic theologians deliberately engaged other religious communities in theological conversation. In effect, the Catholic Church opted to serve humanity in a theological manner. That is, in this world the Church accepted responsibility for the Word of God in the human context. This acceptance raised a significant existential problem for the Catholic Church, which then had to re-define itself in the public forum. This was a challenging undertaking since a religious and political role in the public forum was already well known and accepted by the Church before Vatican II. Yet, even before Vatican II, some theologians recognized that the Church, from a theological perspective, constituted a sacred service, apparently shunning politics, and not engaged in political service as such. A pre-Vatican II theologian has written:

> The chief aim of the Church is to present her authoritative, infallible preaching of the faith, to maintain and preserve

revealed truth, and to dispense supernatural grace by means of the Holy Sacraments. It is her purpose to sanctify in this manner the greatest possible number of human beings in the world, to renew them and thus to lead them to their eternal destiny. In all her dealings with worldly concerns and in the emphasis with which in regard to these she instructs, directs, and commands her faithful children, the Church intends only the advancement of the eternal salvation of souls. She never strives after any political or secular end for the sake of earthly gain or possessions. In her dealings with this world she attempts, as long as the world will agree, to forestall or to settle conflicts that may arise between the Church and State or between Church and Society. She defends her rights and interests as firmly as possible. As far as the word is receptive, she is ready to be of service to the world in the largest possible measure by giving guidance or by mediation (Van de Pol, 1952).

Much has changed theologically since the above was written and a new philosophy, an existential philosophy, is replacing the classical philosophy favoured by Western Catholic theologians. Catholic theologians today must converse, both intellectually and spiritually, with many other communities of religious belief in a global cultural context, Christian and non-Christian. Msgr. Kolbe's (1928) observation about the exclusivity of Catholic philosophy, although accurate in his day, is so no longer. Through cultural advancement other religions have developed their respective philosophies. From the late 19th century onwards some Catholic theologians began abandoning the classical philosophical understanding and accepted an historical understanding and a phenomenological philosophical point of view in their interpretation of experience. This change in perspective, to my mind, has its primary roots in the so-called, and short-lived, Modernist Movement of Western Christianity. In understanding their experiences historically and phenomenologically, many Catholic theologians have abandoned the single cultural norm of Romanism as constituting the ecclesiastical context and have accepted a pluralistic cultural understanding as constituting an ecclesial context. The critical reader will have observed that the term "ecclesial" replaces "ecclesiastical" in my thinking. "Ecclesial" is an intellectual notion arising from phenomenological thinking after Vatican II, whereas "ecclesiastical" is an intellectual concept characteristic of scholastic thinking.

In the contemporary North American context, many theologians seek dialogue partners on the common ground found among the diverse religious traditions. This search for dialogue results, from the virtue of tolerance, as understood in the West. In the American civic tradition tolerance is a significant virtue. But, it can be a curse as well. In fact, in the mind of some theologians, tolerance appears to have fragmented North American culture, rather than unified it. In many theological discussions, a shared vision of life often appears lacking, which makes finding partners for dialogue extremely difficult. It seems clear to me that North American culture lacks an accepted common religious ground about meaning, value and the shared experience of public life. A lack of common ground notwithstanding, Christian believers, even in their pluralistic expression, are readily distinguishable from their counterparts the secular-minded individuals. In current Western society, Christian and secular experience, each provides a *locus* for the interpretation of the believer's experience. Science, the standard interpretive tool of contemporary secular value-system, is a comparatively recent intellectual construction and does not provide answers to the deeper religious and philosophical questions of human understanding. Christian believers, on the other hand, are born into an ecumenical context that is easily distinguished from a secular context. Further, the Western intellectual tradition, from the ancient Greeks onwards, is based on a notion of an abiding and unique *humanum*, which cannot be encompassed by science. Lurie (2000) suggests from a cultural point of view that this *humanum* may be psychologically understood. Further, this psychological understanding enables us to recognize in different cultures a common cultural stage of development in which the same "human psychological nature" is manifested. In classical times, this *humanum* determined the purpose of society and government. It was the purpose of society and government to enhance the human experience by any means within their power. Only in the recent past has this been challenged by the notion of the power of individual sovereignty and the subsequent separation of church and state. To my mind, the devaluing of the *humanum* by the separation of church and state in the public forum can be countered by a proper relationship between the ecclesia and the civil government in the public forum.

However, individual sovereignty, divorced from a community, cannot be an absolute good for the individual believer. An individual believer must be subordinated, in an appropriate manner, to the community. In other words, individuality, not individualism constitutes the proper relationship within the community. From an ecclesial perspective *Gaudium et Spes*, (The Pastoral Constitution on the Church), addresses the mistaken notion of absolute sovereignty and notes that there is no inherent value and meaning in the isolated lives of individuals. Hence, a Christian humanitarianism, incorporating individuality into corporate identity, is founded on human dignity that is ultimately grounded in God's revelation to the community in the person of Jesus of Nazareth. Note that I say humanitarianism, not humanism. The former, within a phenomenological perspective, is a moral understanding in which humans work for the welfare of the human race. Therefore, humanitarian doctrine is not hostile to revelation, as some authorities might still maintain. The latter, humanism, is merely an ethical understanding aiming at right conduct for humanity. Humanism is an intellectual movement that originated during the Renaissance and is rooted in Greek and Roman classical thinking. Humanism emphasizes purely human interests and omits religious interests. It emphasizes the natural world. On the other hand, humanitarianism is open to an *imitatio Christi* (imitation of Christ). An *imitatio Christi* is will become an embodiment of the *humanum*, which secular and humanistic philosophers grasp only partially. The notion of Christian duty, or better Christian responsibility, as an *imitatio Christi* remains based on the belief that something similar to what the medieval theological synthesis attempted to achieve through political conformity, is possible.

It is his or her community to which the individual theologian has a proper responsibility. Thus, theological inquiry, in the modern era, requires a responsible Christian interpretation of the Word of God. The language of modern theological inquiry has ceased to be solely rational and neglectful of the human and social sciences. To their credit, the social sciences are no longer understood in mechanistic terms inherited from the Enlightenment. In contemporary human and social scientific thought, individual subject-centred reason, a classical concept, is replaced by a communal subject-centred understanding, an existential concept, requiring dialogue among a variety of partners, or stakeholders. It is this collective communicative understanding, or rational consciousness, arising from a variety of partners, or stakeholders and, not the propositions of conceptual knowledge, that constitutes the context of an existential theistic theological encounter. In collective communicative understanding, a reconstruction of theism takes place through the interaction of persons, not by a reformulation of propositions, which in fact often brings about no substantial change in meaning.

As noted earlier an existential interpretation is an alternative to the theoretical approach in theology. An existential interpretation does not necessarily mean that theistic theological inquiry reveals a more comprehensive view of the faith. In the contemporary context a theistic existential interpretation provides an appropriate foundation for the spiritual life. This is not to say that the discipline of religious studies cannot assist in the spiritual development of Christian ministers. It is to be noted that the vocation of the Church's ministers, or great the commission, arising from their spiritual life is the cure of souls, the *cure animarum*, intended ultimately for the redemption of the whole community. The redemption of the community is a theistic theological imperative, which cannot be applied to religious studies. The redemptive imperative of theistic theology is realized through an existential theism and is not reserved to particular Christian denominations. Unfortunately, as the history of religious debate has shown, the inter-denominational argument over theological issues since the Reformation has eclipsed the theological imperative of the *cure animarum*.

The theological colleges, which were originally set up to serve the interests of the denominational Churches engaged in debating theological questions, have taken on an independent existence in the modern world. Many of them have separated themselves from their confessional traditions. Philip Hughes (1947) commenting on the effects of the French Revolution on the academic status of the Church writes:

> Another grave loss was the disappearance of all the universities. They had been Catholic, and often papal foundations. In all of them there had been a faculty of theology.... Now they were gone, and when restored they would be restored as State universities, academics for the exploration and exposition of natural truths alone. Education, the formation of the Catholic mind in the new Catholic Europe, would suffer immeasurably, and religious formation to be its intellectual development an extra, something added on.... The leaders of Catholic thought would not be the professional thinkers whom a university produces, but technicians, those to whom the important work

of training the future clergy is committed and who, among other things, teach them theology.

In modern times, and mostly for clinical pastoral purposes, the behavioural sciences have come to dominate theological education. Classical philosophy has been abandoned as a foundational philosophy for theological inquiry. A further complication within the academic climate since the Second World War is that in Western theism there has been an alliance between the evangelical religions and North American style politics. This alliance has introduced a new perspective into theistic theological interpretation. Given the focus by some evangelicals on material prosperity in this life, some theologians view this theistic interpretation as antithetical to the understanding that God's kingdom is not of this world. This combined evangelical and political theistic theological development may be due to the fact that North American Churches operate on a voluntary financial support system as opposed to a governmental established financial support system. Thus, they must realize their own temporal growth independently of the state, which, in some cases, can be counterproductive to their responsibility for the Word of God.

As to its purpose, contemporary theistic theological development, when not constricted by any denominational context, may be critically examined on three grounds. First, it may be critically examined as an academic undertaking rather than practical formation, or praxis. That is, theological development may be examined according to a speculative vs. an existential process. Secondly, it may be critically examined with respect to the apparent loss of faith on the part of believers and, thirdly, critically examined with respect to its failure to cultivate a positive ecclesial consciousness that assists in the spiritual growth of the believer. The spiritual growth of the believer is a primary purpose of theistic theological development. A merely intellectual understanding of theism is a secondary consideration in any theistic theological development. Spiritual growth is fundamental to all theistic theological development. It must be acknowledged that the church's minister is responsible then for enhancing the spirituality of others through ministry. Ministry, in the context of spiritual growth, is to be understood from the perspective of experiencing God's saving presence. However, the recent shift from theory (*theoria*) to existence (*praxis*) in theistic education has caused ministry to become more concerned with the practical understanding of God, rather than the saving power of God's Word. Among the more influential scientific sub-disciplines in North America effecting this change has been that of psychology.

Theistic development, for effective ministry, rests on two presuppositions. One is that the outcome of theological development is more comprehensive than the mere goal of theistic knowledge. In attaining the insights of an existential understanding, as well as a certain theistic erudition, the theologian becomes aware of a transcendental dimension in which the positive sciences assist in the interpretation of the transcendental experience. However, even though philosophical understanding and insights of the social sciences may be mastered within theistic enquiry, they are not to replace theistic theological enquiry. Such replacement by the social sciences impoverishes theism. It seems to me that much theistic theological study in the North American seminaries, of all the denominations, has been replaced by training and acquisition of particular skills needed for leadership in contemporary Christian communities. As a result many theologians have come to depend increasingly on the secular academy in place of a faith community as a reference group. Further, a significant particular issue in theistic development is the question of which community is addressed by the gospels in their literary form. This issue is further complicated by the addition of the community's local historical and legal texts. Another complicating presupposition is that a mature theistic development is required on the part of the minister, which is the *sine qua non* of effective ministry. A mature theism, then, discloses that unless God is the primary minister working through the theologian the work undertaken will not bear proper fruit. Nor will such work disclose a proper responsibility for the Word of God. Christian theism divorced from prayer is deficient in human meaning.

My theistic theological development is directed towards the formation of my mind, being conformed to the mind of Christ, such that my way of praying and believing becomes one. The theism that arises from the interpretation of my experience of God is personal, but not private, and reveals opportunities for future transcendental encounters. Thus, a mere philosophy of religion, then, is inadequate to reveal my spiritual centre where my belief and prayer are united. Although, Heni Bergson (1944) suggests that philosophy introduces one to the spiritual life. It shows that at the same time the relation of the life of the spirit to that of the body, he also notes. In this respect Pastoral Psychology and Counselling, rooted in the study of religion, address my emotional centre, not my spiritual centre. On the contrary, a theistic theological inquiry, which engages my spirit in dialogue with God's revelation, addresses my spiritual centre. Further, it must be remembered that even crisis counselling with its emotional benefits cannot replace a pastoral theology that is intended to assist believers in understanding their experience and help them order their lives around their spiritual centre.

Christian theistic theological reflection has a dual origin. It arises from the reflection on the life of Jesus of Nazareth and on the community's shared consciousness of that life. Initially this theological reflection was a sharing of ideas by those believers most disposed to learning, as opposed to religious piety. In its early historical development theistic theological reflection, as opposed to religious piety, took the form of a commentary on the scriptures of the Old and New Testaments. Only later did believers pose questions arising from their personal experience in light of the interpretation of the scriptures. The questions that eventually arose from collective and individual experiences within the faith community necessarily gave rise to a theistic theological system of interpretation, which depended upon a classical philosophy. In the West, the acceptance of Aristotle's philosophy, as a basis for theistic theological interpretation, effected a change in direction from the earlier folklore, legends and epics that structured religious understanding. Eventually, folklore, legends and epics that structured religious understanding developed into the theistic theological interpretation, which became characteristic of the academy. The Aristotelian approach prepared the way for the dominance of scholastic tradition in Western theology where the application of reason triumphed. In later historical development, Platonic and Augustinian ways of thinking introduced a different direction and structure into theistic theological thinking. The juxtaposition of Aristotelian and Platonic-Augustinian thought led to a situation in which knowledge gained through abstract reason about God's creation, that is, through Aristotelian philosophy, was contrasted with knowledge that was gained through a personal loving relationship with God, that is, through a Platonic–Augustinian philosophy.

The direct stimulus for this brief book is the unfinished theistic theological business of the late nineteenth and early twentieth centuries. This unfinished theological business is the legacy of the philosophers and theologians living at the time of the so-called Modernist crisis. The Modernist crisis challenged the dominant scholastic theological view that had characterized Christian theology since the Middle Ages. Official Catholic ecclesiastical opposition was very strong and as a result, the movement was terminated within the Catholic Church and thus had no future life among Catholic theologians. Enlightened theologians, however, resisted the Roman Catholic Church's suppression of Modernist theology, as did the critical theologians of other denominations. Ironically, today, Catholic theology has expanded the positive results of the critical scholarship that originated during the time of this movement. The contemporary Christian theistic theological climate facilitates a critical ecumenical theology. Although there is a move, in some quarters, to include non-Christians in the ecumenical context, a truly ecumenical theism is an "in-house" theism. And being one that is common to the Christian household it is based on a reflection on the life of Jesus as experienced within the various Christian communities. The Canadian Conference of Catholic Bishops (2009) however, teaches that ecumenism, in a broader sense, also involves working for better relations with Judaism, Islam and other non-Christian religions. Within Christian communities there is a growing trend to an existential approach in pastoral theistic interpretation. In this existential approach the noetic notion of intersubjectivity, that is, the mind's understanding of intersubjectivity, replaces the rational ideal of objectivity in the development of modern theistic theological thought. Modern theism, proposes an existential relationship between creature and creator, understood not as something developing in a vacuum, but as developing in the context of God's personal initiative calling persons into existence and inviting into them to an everlasting relationship. It is this initiative of God which evokes a response from the faithful which is most suitably interpreted from a phenomenological point of view.

Theism is a *ministerium verbi divini,* that is, a service to the word of God. I understand this service as a broader concept than that of traditional Christian understanding. It includes service to the Word of God that is undertaken in Hebrew and Islamic revelation as well. Thus, the *ministerium verbi divini* is not a view mediated solely through an understanding of the temporal and resurrected life of Jesus of Nazareth. It incorporates thinking from Jewish and Muslim philosophies in their own right. Further, such service to the Word of God as a ministry takes into account the service of an individual to the community, as well, not just to the Word of God. It must be remembered, however, that in this understanding, neither the community nor the individual are primarily to be served by theistic theological interpretation, but God receives the primary service. This service rendered for God's sake, from a Jewish, Christian and Muslim perspective is prompted by the revelation to these communities. This revelation is subsequently understood through prayerful interpretation. A further question, then, arises in the mind of the critical thinker: Can such service be rendered to God outside of the traditional monotheistic understanding of revelation? Or, the same question put from within a Christian perspective, can those outside the Church do proper theistic theology? Again, put otherwise, is being within the visible church a necessary prerequisite for theistic theology? Many Catholic Christians see the Invisible Church in the Visible Church and mysteriously related to it, yet not as simply identical or co-extensive with it. Further, some of the faithful believe that there are many individuals within the Visible Church that do not belong to the Invisible Church; and there are many individuals not within the Visible Church that belong to the Invisible Church. This belief arose out of the Modernist crisis mentioned above. In attending to the Word of God, Christian theologians and religious philosophers incorporate the *ministerium verbi divini* into their ministry and thus are effective. What I say here about the Christian experience is to be understood, *inter alia*, as applicable to the Jewish and Muslim faith communities, as well.

Historically, Western religious philosophy is linked to Hellenism, which gave rise to the Socratic method and the dialectic of Plato. Certain religious thinkers, called Apologists, were the first Catholic intellectuals, converts from Paganism and the Philosophical religions by whose constructive work the Church comes unembarrassed by any temporary alliance with the instability of merely human theorising (Hughes, 1947). Thus, the Socratic methodology and the dialectic of Plato became the basis for the philosophical thinking of the Christian Church. Further, at the beginning of the 20th Century Western faith communities began to use psychology, the new science, to explain the human condition and humanity's religious experience. The discovery of psychoanalysis subsequently brought about a change in almost every philosophical point of view within these communities. The earlier writings of the psychoanalyst Alfred Adler (1870-1937), a contemporary of Sigmund Freud, are clearly rooted in philosophical thinking. Today, psychological thinking has replaced much philosophical thinking in the interpretation of religious experience. Notwithstanding this, I write philosophically from a phenomenological perspective recognizing that "conscious intent" is critical to any religious philosophy. Western philosophers have acknowledged that the Natural Law Theory has historically formed the basis of much religious philosophical thinking but that same philosophy is now being abandoned by many of their successors. Further, the Quantum theory in physics, as well as phenomenological philosophy have challenged the Natural Law Theory as relevant to contemporary human experience.

In place of the Natural Law Theory, a new notion of the understanding of being and reality is disclosed through a phenomenological philosophy. However, it is to be acknowledged that this new understanding this new understanding of being and reality, as consciously purposive activity, was contained within limits, in pre-Cartesian philosophy. Monsignor Kolbe's observations about this are worth noting, given our present context. After Martin Luther, Kolbe (1928) notes came:

Descartes, who, with the best intentions, for he was a devout Catholic, thought he could re-express all Philosophy from his own speculations. Among other things, he taught that the soul governed the body from without like an engine-driver....After that the old philosophy, though still taught in the Catholic Colleges, came to be by the "modernist" world looked upon as extinct....But Descartes is dethroned, and the new school of Catholic Philosophy is now absorbing all the experience of the last four centuries and is restating the old solutions of the world's problems in modern ways.

Under certain conditions and, within limited autonomy, intellectual freedom allows an individual to make a conscious choice in existential action. In the past, some Western philosophers have recognized this contextually determined freedom. They noted that there is a hierarchy of values in experience and that the conscious choice on the part of the subject depends on a variety of subordinate causal relationships. One's conscious choice, or purposiveness, requires causal relationships within human experience. Classical philosophers have noted that, of itself, created nature is neutral or value-free. It is human choice, or intent, that assigns value to created nature. Thus, individuals assign value to their experience, natural or supernatural. Within this understanding, historically, individuals who believe in the Judeo-Christian religious perspective accept the doctrine of a "fallen nature" as a moral value, which affects their understanding of all life, human, angelic and divine.

I have been discussing, if somewhat eclectically, theistic theological enquiry as a responsibility for the Word of God. Below I review such responsible understanding under three headings that arise from my general reading and discussions with other professionals. These discussions concerned the understanding of phenomenological philosophy within their respective disciplines and professional contexts.

Over time it became apparent to me that the ways of thinking that these individuals inherited were often no longer satisfactory in their professional lives. Thus, many of us, including me, began to re-think our faith experience. This lack of satisfaction confronts many today within a variety of disciplines. For Catholics in particular, Vatican II signalled the end of conventional Western theism. As a result, my colleagues and I recognized that Vatican II was not a mere up-dating of doctrine and dogma. Rather, it is one stage in an evolution that is occurring within Catholic theistic theological thinking.

III THE EXISTENTIAL SITUATION
IN WHICH I FIND MYSELF

I am living in a culture that has not been envisioned or brought about merely by one individual or by many individuals. Rather, my present culture is determined by many factors. Indeed, my present culture may even be over-determined by many factors. By that I mean no one factor can be held solely responsible for the direction of its development. I am likely not to see my present situation as it develops until it is too late for me to significantly effect its direction. The truth is that my culture happens to me whether I like it or not. I cannot stop it. Yet, I am personally involved, even though minimally, in its transformation as it now takes place. My present cultural situation is that I live within the anxiety and tensions that accompany the end of conventional Western Christianity. But within this tension there are indications of a new beginning and a new future. As a Christian, I must determine this future within my community and in collaboration with all of the churches and other faith groups, as well.

In the West, soon after the Second World War, a shift in religious understanding in what is theologically sacred and, in what philosophically constitutes a person, took place. Significantly, this shift, which is still occurring today, continues to signal a change in philosophical and theistic theological thinking. The primacy of the collective is giving way to the primacy of the individual. In the modern era the notion of the sacred is no longer based on a rural civilisation and monarchical society, which shaped the medieval church's governing structures. The shape of the modern church's governing structures is now determined by industrial civilisation and democratic society. Given the contemporary governing structure of the Church those who are not adherents of the visible church may enjoy the social benefits of its activity but they are not direct sharers in its spiritual activity. This does not mean, however, that those outside the visible limits of the Church are not, in some manner, within the Church, even if mysteriously. It is sometimes argued, by theologians, that the true church in each generation may even be found with those who have been excommunicated from the actual visible Church. This view is not that unorthodox when we realize that the truth of the Church's creed is to be tested by its practical value in promoting spiritual life and growth in the understanding of the believer. In Western society at large, it seems to me, that a new form of theistic understanding is coming to birth. As he or she rejects the traditional form of theistic understanding the contemporary Christian knows that the faith of the believer develops within contemporary communities capable of rediscovering the sources of the evangelical inspiration of the scriptures.

It is readily recognized by the critical thinker that Christianity has no cosmology of its own. However, unlike the Christian religious tradition, pagan religious traditions have mythologies and legends, which explain and interpret their understanding of religious experience. Paganism has no fixed creed of belief (Hughes, 1947). Nor does paganism have among its public figures martyrs giving up their lives for a moral law. Christianity, on the contrary, bases its reflections on the spirituality of the human inner experience contextualized within various cultures. Christian liberal theology within the Catholic tradition dated from 1789 – 1878 by Hughes (1947) has for its subject the human experience. In the case of Christian liberal theology the historical and written records of the church are secondary in the interpretation of religious experience. Theologians consult these traditional records for orthodox interpretation, but only the reflection on the religious experience itself provides the true subject matter. Thus, liberal Christian theology belongs to the category of human experience, not to the category of statement, which is the category of traditional scholastic theology does

In my encounter with God and, since I am an intelligent being according the Henri Bergson (1944), I transcend the boundaries of my creaturely existence in such a way that I become more truly and authentically myself. This type of encounter in which boundaries are transcended is not for mystics only. This encounter is the centre of the Christian life. I come to know God as I know any other person, that is, through mutual self-giving. On my part, this requires a distinction between philosophical and theistic theological effort. Philosophical and theistic theological interpretation of revelation differs. Philosophical interpretation inquires into revelation as a cognitive possibility, whereas, theistic theological interpretation inquires into the historicity of revelation as an event. Note that I do not say the historicism of revelation. Further discussion on the philosophical significance of the suffixes "-ism" and "-ity" occurs in a later chapter. There are limits to the use of philosophy in my approach to the mystery of God. As with any personal relationship, a personal encounter with God defies total objectivity. Mystical communion, on the other hand, is a subjective experience of being-with, which transcends the conventions of my earthly existence. I cannot authentically know others unless I know them as persons, not as objects and, certainly not as virtual reality. As well, God must be incorporated into my understanding of the human person because should I take the understanding of God out of that understanding I take away what is authentically humanitarian in me.

The writer of prose may author a story of mystery and intrigue without being in the actual situation or context of intrigue. In writing prose the author has a certain freedom and creativity not permitted to the philosopher whose existential condition, the actual situation, determines philosophical thinking. The existential conditions affect a particular philosophical perspective. The poet, on the other hand, does not possess the literary freedom of the prose author, nor is the poet hampered by the existential restrictions of the philosopher. The poet transcends both. In short, the poet creates poetry, which touches on the deeper constitution of the human being and not just sense experience and reason. Poetry is able to evoke a deeper level of meaning than the merely conscious level of a rational interpretation. From a psychological, as well as a phenomenological philosophical perspective in the minds of some, it may be argued that human beings who lack a poetic understanding are in danger of being alienated from their deeper and authentic selves. Such persons are, it may be contended, in danger of becoming identified with functions others have determined for them. In other words, expressed in contemporary technological terms, the danger is not that in the future machines and computers may become like humans but, rather, that humans may become like machines or computers. This is the existential situation in which I find myself and in which I must then make my contribution theologically to my culture as an individual in society.

Theology at the Service of the Individual in Community

For many of us our experience is that we are estranged from the religion we inherited. I maintain that this problem has been generated through our experience and is due to the end of conventional Christianity and the death of the traditional understanding of God. That is, the traditional philosophical conventions we designed to protect us from anxiety have been shown to be inadequate in the modern world. In their place we have developed new cultural and philosophical safeguards. However, the usefulness of these new safeguards has been proven to be relative and not universal. Those of the faithful who are prepared and able to form their own judgment in religious matters depend on the adequacy of the philosophy of their culture. This dependency poses a problem for Christian philosophers and theologians. The outcomes of the interpretation of the Gospel message, through philosophy and theistic theology, are not solely the products of culture. Yet, conventional Christian interpretations of the Gospel are largely a product of culture. Albert Nolan (1978) observed that the early Christians simply adapted Jesus' prophecy to the new set of circumstances in which they found themselves. Inherited forms of religious expression, conceptions, and customs, as well as Christianity's spirit and mentality are rooted in the world of a Greco-Roman-Germanic civilization. Once the message had been taken outside Palestine with its particular political crisis, and more especially once the Romans had destroyed the Jewish nation, it was felt that the message had to be adapted to other situations or indeed to any and every situation (Nolan, 1978). Today, the plurality of inherited forms of expression and customs is so much a part of Western civilization that profound changes to this plural pattern of culture necessarily influence conventional Christianity. Within the plurality of contemporary culture Christian churches have become secularised social institutions. That is, humans, not God, have become the measure, thus reversing the traditional understanding of God as being the measure of all things. Human beings, created in the image and likeness of God, seek existential theological understanding in our modern era. Such theistic theological understanding is to be found in service to a transcendent reality revealed through human existence.

I admit that Catholic theistic theology springs from the need to supply an intellectual embodiment and expression, as opposed to relying on folklore and myth, for the interpretation of religious experience. In supplying this embodiment theologians interpret the Church's teaching in harmony with the mind of the age. The interpretation of revealed religion is an ever-varying expression of religious experience. The earlier scholastic Catholic theology comprises a doctrinal system and a construct of human understanding. It is an intelligible construction, not of poetical, but of theological, philosophical, ethical, scientific and historical beliefs and conceptions, which the spirit of Christ has inspired. This way of thinking has its genesis in an intelligible way of being-in-faith, that is, a theological being-in-faith. Theistic theological construction presupposes that human experience incorporates the natural desire to know. The desire to know is a movement toward God by an intelligent being who is destined for God. Such a philosophical attitude on the part of the believing inquirer leads to personal self-discovery, that is, to seeing for oneself and to doing for oneself. One of the tasks the theologian performs is to seek clarification concerning the intersubjectivity, which exists between God as a knowing subject and the human being as a knowing subject. Given the intersubjective relationship which is perpetually developing some philosophers are inclined to conclude that theology can never complete this task of clarification.

The theologian must remain in close contact with the hopes and the anguish of his or her own age employing the philosophy most suitable to the times and the lived experience of believers. It is highly doubtful that scholasticism remains the most suitable philosophy for the majority of the faithful. Only by remaining in close contact with the Christian tradition can the theologian speak in a meaningful way. Today, there is need to establish a philosophy that will be suitable to our need of giving expression to the theistic theological meaning of God's revelation to a humanity-as-subject. Experience has shown that the outcome of theistic theological reflection has an influence on the moral and social life of individuals in community. Further, history shows us that all substantial deepening of theistic theological understanding has been the work not of ecclesiastical officials, but of faithful individuals, sometimes in opposition to ecclesiastical officials, whose proper role is to correct and modify the formal teaching of the Church. This modification is in keeping with Auguste Sabatier's (2003) understanding that it is not enough that theology makes clear the senility of the old forms of religion; its task is to create if for new forms, he reminds his readers. In my experience, theistic theology and revelation act and react upon each other. My experience is that theistic theological interpretation grows in my intellectual understanding, whereas, revelation unfolds within my conscious experience.

Natural theistic theology, as a discipline, lies outside the Catholic tradition. Catholic theologians regard natural theistic theology more as a philosophy than a theology. In fact, some theologians have never considered that it had a proper responsibility to interpret revelation. It is the epistemological philosopher's proper responsibility to inquire into knowledge, not revelation. Natural theistic theology operates outside revelation. The *sensus fidelium*, that is, the sense of the faithful, is concerned with the Church's life. Theologians are required to interpret the *sensus fidelium*. Even in this role theologians are not central to church's life. However, they are essential to the church's development of doctrine. The Church could get along without theologians but it could not get along without the *sensus fidelium*. The *sensus fidelium* is a lived sense of the faith in the presence of the Holy Spirit that requires, at minimum, two other factors that allow the *sensus fidelium*, to develop. These two factors are theologians, as individuals, and the Magisterium, that is, the collective teaching authority of the Church.

At the beginning of the 20th Century, controversial issues in theological interpretation in the American Church were usually contested at the level of pastoral or practical theology. By contrast theological interpretation in France and much of the Continent was conducted at the level of theoretical and existential theology. The problem was that the French theologians and, many of the Continental theologians, could not understand the non-metaphysical language or practical thought of the Americans. The European theologians tended to regard such thought as heretical. In their praxis, the American theologians believed themselves to be faithful in interpreting the *sensus fidelium*. On the Continent and in England, liberal Catholics sought to separate the new scientific knowledge from the teaching authority of the Roman Church. At its worst, according to Philip Hughes (1947) Liberalism denied the right of the Catholic Church to be a religious system having views on the morality of public life. The Modernists, however, were not true liberalists, but rather, a loose group of thinkers who sought to reconcile the conflict between the Church and new scientific knowledge by up-dating the meaning of dogma and Church authority. The Modernist understanding I argue, became the forerunner of the notion of *aggiornamento* of Vatican II. For the French and Italian Modernists, such as, Henri Bergson, Alfred Loisy, Henri Bremond and Romolo Murri, Abbate Cavallanti and Ernesto Buonaiuti, a life of study followed naturally upon a life of prayer. For them the saintly life, of necessity, preceded the doctrine of the theologian. The relationship between prayer and study is a perennial issue in the spiritual growth of the believer. Theologians convene to serve the spiritual needs of the individual in community, as well. Such convening often occurs across different denominations. Because of this convening across denominational lines I suggest that the lines of cleavage in Christendom are becoming less clearly drawn between denominations. Existential issues, which are less demarcated, are replacing theoretical confessional controversies.

Even allowing for the spiritual growth of the believer, the development of theological understanding has remained to a large degree an activity of the institutional Church. Formal theistic theological interpretation has deep roots stretching into inter-testamental times. The development of theistic theology in the Gentile-Christian Church arose from the belief that the conception of God as the Father of Christ, and of Christ as the Son of God, must be demonstrated as a universal truth of reason based on a Hellenic philosophical understanding. In the contemporary ecumenical climate, theistic theology, as a human discipline, must take into account all religious phenomena, not just Christian phenomenon. Such accounting makes theology a labour of human reason, which recognizes revelation as a gift from God, at least this is so from the Christian perspective. Still, it must be remembered that theology is an after thought in the understanding of human experience. That is, theology is a product of reflection, not of revelation. From an existential perspective it matters little that Christianity has developed in Roman and Protestant forms since the existential context is common to both. Christians participate in the transition to a new cultural expression and practice of the faith when developing an existential theology. To my mind, an existential philosophy establishes the parameters for the formation of a contemporary common ground that could bring about the decline of the theological antithesis between Rome and the Reformation. Further, it is possible that the decline of the theological antithesis between Rome and the Reformation could result in a new Christian understanding which would be neither Roman nor Reformed. This presents an exciting opportunity for existential theologians whose perspective derives from the Modernist mind-set.

Christianity without Christ is not a new Christianity but a new social ideal. Christianity with a mystical, but no historical Christ, is not a new Christianity but another religion. Further, Christianity with Christ as a moral ideal, but not worthy of worship, is not a new Christianity, but an adaptation of Christian teaching to other religious or moral systems.

In Christian theology teachings that reduce the scriptural Christ to a social Christ are not proper theological teachings at all. They are social substitutions. This observation notwithstanding, theistic theologians must make fresh interpretations in each age otherwise they has no reason for existence. However, with the inordinate emphasis on the private needs of the contemporary individual there is a danger that the Church may be seen as unnecessary in the development of the theistic theological and spiritual life. Yet, it is through the Church that new generations are introduced to the Christian faith. It must not be forgotten that the primary task of the theologian is the analysis of the public and communal revelation in the experience of the Church collectively and of the individual believer and not an analysis of particular and individual economic, sociological or psychological experiences.

Modern philosophy must be an existential undertaking if it is to support contemporary theology. Tertullian, who died c. 225 AD, based himself on the "natural man" who was simple, rude, uncultured and untaught and not ruined by Greek education. He understood the natural man to be *anima naturaliter Christiana*. Tertullian invited the faithful to return to their personal religious experience since it was prior to any theory about their experience. In this approach he explored the spiritual life in order to find the Christian understanding of God. Socrates, as a philosophical thinker, desired to help clarify the thinking of poets, politicians as well as whomever he met in market place, young and old, uneducated or uneducated. In his endeavour, Socrates did not initiate a system of philosophy. Rather, he undertook a responsible approach to thinking. Some Twentieth Century thinkers, Thomas Altizer, Gabriel Vahanian, Paul van Buren and others have concluded that God has died in the mass technological culture of the nineteenth century. Although not dead, it is true that God may be perceived as absent from us. God has been perceived as absent before. But God has returned in the past and God may return in the future, as it were, making use of new images and new symbols. Making use of new images and new symbols is the proper task of existential philosophers and theologians. New images and new symbols will reveal that the faithful cannot do without the religious philosopher as theologians articulate ideas and express them in a language that reflects contemporary culture.

The theistic theological task today is conceived differently than it was in the days of the all-encompassing Medieval theological systems. Historical criticism shows that a change in philosophy precedes a change in theology. Since, in the Western context, at least change in philosophy precedes change in theology, this is a perennial state of affairs and there can be no final philosophy or theology. The task of the contemporary theologian is to make known the abiding truths of Christianity as well as the truth in all revealed religions. The principle usefulness of the theologian is to satisfy the inquiries of the believer and address any troubles arising within the faith. However, the principle usefulness of the pastoral counselor is to address troubles arising within the spirit. To my mind, a proper theistic theology, in fact, can address both. For a theistic theology to be proper and satisfy the believer's conviction it must reflect a personal confession of faith. To be proper and satisfy the believer is a demand from within, not from without, the individual. This life from within is culturally conditioned and theistic theology serves to assist the faithful in interpreting this cultural conditioning within the community.

IV CHRISTIAN CULTURE:
ITS PHILOSOPHICAL ROOTS
AND PRESENT CRISIS

The Aims and the Assumptions of Christian Culture

Culture is an intelligible pattern of life, which influences the aims and habits of individuals and has been created collectively by them. The Western European culture with its set of outlooks, aims and ways of life has been transmitted to other parts of the world resulting in both positive and negative effects. Culture includes, in my understanding, the official societies and associations that address the interests of various populations and are vital to their physical, political and spiritual existence. Those cultural activities that enrich life must also preserve or augment that life. The understanding of culture that I examine includes all these official societies and associations.

Serious inquirers often mistakenly think that the culture in which we presently live is of necessity a part of the nature of things. Culture is not natural, but fabricated or fashioned, by humans. Henri Bergson (1944) suggests the same for philosophy which must go counter to the bent of the intellect. Culture needs tending like a garden or the soil. Three influences which mould a culture are: a) its dogmas, that is, that which a culture takes for granted about itself, b) its rituals, that is, the things its populace does every day, and c) its structure and organization of social life, that is, interpersonal and corporate relationships. Theologians are beginning to recognize that the traditional culture of European civilization is outdated to the point of uselessness. Thus, other cultures, of an entirely different fabrication and fashion, are beginning to take its place. There are movements within modern European culture that are proving to be preferred to the movements of Europe's traditional cultural life. Two such movements are, one, the denial of metaphysical being or the denial of an ontology, classically understood, and two, the acceptance of science, technology and reason as possessing ultimate control over things and human beings. However, science, technology and reason, in themselves, do not give control over, nor determine things or human beings. As well, industrialism, not industrialization, has introduced the improper use of the machine, which has led to depersonalization. It was once hoped that industrialization being the proper approach would give the mass population what had been the privilege of the upper economic classes.

Since the replacement of a proper industrialization, by industrialism, the improper approach, it is becoming clear that any new shape of a believing community ought not to be patterned on any model of industrialism. Within the West, Christian culture was originally conceived not so much as learning a lesson about the faith, but as an initiation into a new life, or as an initiation into the mystery of life. Christian culture is something that cannot be conveyed by words alone, but is conveyed by that which involves a disciplined activity of the whole person. Christian culture requires more than catechesis. It is a process of catharsis and illumination which is centred in the sacred mysteries and, which is subsequently embodied in symbolism and liturgical action. It is in the activity of worship that the Christian culture originates and develops. Insofar as the conception of worship differs there is also a difference in the conception of culture and vice versa. A culture lacking a form of worship cannot transform society.

As a believer, I require a culture, not a theistic theology, to make sense of my life in narrative terms, which may be myth, folklore or legend. I require a theistic theology, not culture, to make sense of my life in spiritual terms, which is an intelligible philosophical approach. As a Christian my intelligible theistic theological understanding, or philosophical understanding, is disclosed within the immediate experience of my life in the spirit. What is the spirit of God revealing to me now, I may ask. This is a theistic theological question, not a cultural one. Culture is not theology. The uncritical acceptance of a religious life in terms of myth and folklore cannot address this question intelligibly, although it may address it socially. Thus, theistic theology's purpose in the public sphere, that is, the community at large, does not serve the same purpose as religion in one's life. Theistic theology and religion in one's life each fulfill different roles in a pluralistic society. Theologians need to rethink theology in the public square. Since theological opinions arise in a pluralistic society I need to ask the question: Do theologians within a single religious context differ from theologians within a pluralistic religious context? The distinction between single and pluralistic religious contexts opens at least three areas of discussion concerning the status of theistic theology. The first area: theistic theology, as a service to a religion based on myth or folklore, seems to be in decline. The second area: theistic theology, as descriptive and normative in contemporary civil society needs to be acknowledged as a discipline and clarified as to intent and third, theistic theology as a source for integration and of social division needs to be reappraised.

As many Christians realize today, the Church is no longer the moral guardian of the community in contemporary society. There has been a shift in emphasis from the guardianship responsibility of the corporation to the responsibility of the individual member for his or her moral life. I consider this shift from propositional truth, a corporate principle, to personal truth, an individual experience, not as an actual a decline but merely a highly significant change. Such change simply means a re-alignment of our ways of thinking appropriate to our time and culture. In the West, the move has been to phenomenological understanding in which a new relationship, between theistic theology and the contemporary world, is reflected. Within this change, theistic theology takes on a new responsibility in interpreting revelation for contemporary believers. In this new interpretive context theistic theological belief may or may not be affected by secularization. Note that I do not say secularism. Secularization, not secularism, is characteristic of the new phase of service-orientated and information-based economies that are replacing the industrial-based economics in influencing theological thought. Hence, under the right conditions in this new context of secularization the theologian's discursive power in the public square may come to exceed traditional institutional power. In a word, theistic theology, like the economy, is information-based, not industry-based, as it were, and there will be an increase in the tension between an individual theologian's interpretation, information-based, and that of the Magisterium, industrial-based. Thus, there is need for an appropriate modern philosophy to support contemporary theistic theology in its new social context.

Civil society is a philosophical idea that was conceived in contrast to the ideas of the natural and hierarchical orders of the classical era. In that era, it was accepted that God sanctioned the natural order and the hierarchical order. In such a society the human, or acquired, virtues were contrasted with the theological or revealed virtues. Upon the theological, or revealed, virtues is founded a religious humanitarianism that aspires to a higher human good that constitutes our Christian culture. In our contemporary culture fundamentalist theology, is adverse to a wider social engagement with the public forum. Whereas, evangelical theology engages the entire public forum as the *locus* of Christ's redeeming activity. Given the apparent growth in evangelical theology, I make the general observation, that Western theology's influence on culture is moving from the public square expressed as the state, its traditional *locus*, to the public square of civil society, its contemporary *locus*.

V RECONSTRUCTION IN THEISTIC THEOLOGY

The task of theology and of the theologian is a temporary one no matter in what age he or she lives. It would be a distinct loss given the work of the theologian if he or she should be so out of sympathy with the church's history so as to lose the theological continuity of Christian generations. In our time within this theological continuity, collective personal experience trumps individual personal experience. Thus, an isolated Christian confession of faith is a contradiction. I note that Christian revelation does not claim to give answers to questions of human curiosity. The reverse is true. Human curiosity about revelation requires theological answers. Without access to all the answers Christian theologians work out a view of God and the world within the context of revelation. One of the greatest dangers to the philosopher/theologian in our time is found in the ability to defend, more or less successfully, any philosophical and theological position brought to our awareness. Sophisticated thinkers persuade themselves that what they want to believe is true, or that all philosophical and theological convictions are more or less justified.

It seems to me that, for many today, theistic theology has lost its hold on the believer's intellect and religious activities. But often theistic theology retains its hold on the believer's sentimental or pietistic life. Contemporary scientific, technological and cosmological understanding has undermined theological thinking such that it has ceased to be of use to the believer. Therefore, a contemporary theistic theological reconstruction must not uncritically adapt to the current scientific, technological and cosmological understanding prevalent in the contemporary anti-religious age. Rather, any contemporary theistic theological reconstruction must originate in a properly criticized living faith. Contemporary theistic theological reconstruction is due to the impulse, within the person, of intelligent life. This impulse ultimately results in a personal confession of faith. And there are certain convictions in the modern era that arise from a personal confession of faith that may be philosophically examined. These convictions are: one, that divine immanence reflects a denial of the separation of the sacred and secular; and, two, that the development of a religious and social consciousness suggests that we are all members of one another in some manner of union; and, three, that religious psychology addresses personal activity, of the body and of the mind, which constitutes the person. However, convictions arising from scientific formulations and theological formulations are subjective statements reflecting experience that may be doubted. Science, by the terms it sets for it problems, seeks only the causal connections of phenomena already there, and therefore excludes questions of ultimate origin and destiny. Thus for the contemporary religious thinker a reconstructed theistic theology is required to address these latter questions.

The most significant outcome of the Western-style developing culture in our time is the sense of the value of the individual person. Theistic theologians recognize this deepening sense of the value of the person. Further, it is recognized by astute theologians that the old dualism of justice and love, or holiness and love, causes confusion in both morality and theology. It is often felt that, in contemporary experience, there is division in God, that nature, law, and grace have different purposes instead of all working toward the same end. Some of us know through our experience that religious belief and higher poetry bring us nearer to God, as it were, than abstract metaphysics. Deepening our acquaintance with God is the one supreme purpose of the Christian life. Each new stage of an acquaintance of God reflects a deepening personal relationship of divine friendship. In accepting this view my understanding of theology changes. Thus, my theistic theology needs to be reconstructed accordingly. The continued separation of the moral and the theological becomes increasingly impossible. My moral life is one of the main *loci* of a theistic theological view. And I can conceive of no salvation that does not include my philosophical and theological character, which needs to be reconstructed.

SECTION TWO

VI THRESHOLDS OF PHENOMENOLOGICAL THEOLOGICAL INQUIRY

Phenomenological Philosophical Inquiry

Phenomenological theological inquiry concerns itself with physical existence and the theological metaphysics that has traditionally been described as the "Queen of the Sciences." However, according to Auguste Sabatier (2003), the question is no longer of theology being the queen of the other sciences, but whether the other sciences will accept her as their sister. About the purpose of a phenomenological theological inquiry, Dermot Moran (2005) notes that phenomenological theology seeks to reach "God without God", a phrase coined by Husserl. To reach God without God is the missing intent in the holism of J. C. Smuts according to Msgr. Kolbe. According to him, Smuts considers that the idea of God cannot be inferred from the visible world and may therefore be ignored in a discussion of it (Kolbe, 1928). The idea of God, or the Infinite understood from a Catholic philosophical point of view, must be read into Smuts' *Holism and Evolution*, notes Kolbe. The phenomenological theologian makes inquiries into the pre-reflective human understanding of the "natural man" who is similar to that noted by Tertullian above. It is to be remembered that all poets and artists inquire into the same phenomena of pre-reflective understanding. The theistic theological understanding arrived at by the phenomenological method of interpretation of the natural man arises from an existential, not idealistic, attitude towards life. Søren Kierkegaard was among the first to initiate existential inquiry into life, which other philosophers and theologians have followed. Since his particular initiative cannot be investigated in this book, I encourage the reader to investigate his existential philosophical thinking independently.

Phenomenological Thresholds within the Modernist Movement

Modernist thought developed within the theological hermeneutic in Europe and England about 1900 that viewed tradition and dogma as symbolic expressions of religious experience. Modernists insisted upon the importance of religious phenomena as the starting point of a description of an occurrence. George Tyrrell (1861–1909) and Alfred Loisy (1857–1940) were significant representatives of Modernist thinking and their theological criticism consisted of evaluating the inherited symbolic expressions of religious interpretation of their time. Confronted with a modern world, which had evolved outside of Christianity, the official Catholic hierarchy ceased to excommunicate those who held alternative views and began trying to understand them. Modernist theologians, in contrast to classical theologians, wanted to follow the thinking of the creative Western philosophers who sought a *ressourcement*, a return to the sources of revelation and tradition. Such was George Tyrrell's and Alfred Loisy's intent and experience. As a return to the sources of revelation and tradition, *ressourcement* reflects their era and the thrust of their thinking. However, in Tyrrell's thinking there was one important exception. Rather than expect the Church to embrace science, history and change accordingly, Tyrrell expected science and history to embrace revelation through the Church and develop accordingly in the light of Christ. Tyrrell and Loisy lived in the new age of Catholic theological thinking inaugurated by Leo XIII. According to Philip Hughes (1947) Leo XIII was a pope, supremely gifted in political understanding and in the diplomatic approach. Further, he was:

> a traditionalist and a conservative who thought in modern terms and spoke in the modern idiom, and whose long reign is

the beginning of a new age of Catholic history, the age in which we live, an age which as yet is in the state of transition and whose revolutionary character is only beginning to be apparent to us.

Today, to my mind, many Catholic Christians remain at the beginning stage of Tyrrell's spiritual liberation, that is, at the initial stages of theological liberation introduced by the modern world. These initial stages signal the beginning of a significant shift that needs to be popularized and rendered serviceable to believing individuals in contemporary society. For this shift to be serviceable to believing individuals it must confirm the faith and, to be serviceable to theologians it must interpret the faith.

Within the Anglican tradition Modernist theologians are known as "modern churchmen" and the most influential among them were H. D. A. Major and W. R. Inge. Large numbers of these churchmen regarded the claims of Christianity as inconsistent with modern ways of thought. Phrases like the "Fatherhood of God," "salvation through Christ" and "life after death" seemed like meaningless platitudes to them. In short, new theological understandings were required which were intended to prepare the way for the future of belief. Thus, within the Anglican communion, theological thinking took on a new philosophical form of existential phenomenology. A Roman Catholic lay theologian, Leslie Dewart (1966) inquired into the de-hellenization of doctrine and dogma through a critical philosophical approach to theological reconstruction. De-hellenization, as an effort at theological reconstruction, is a philosophical phenomenological interpretive activity, which replaces the classical philosophical method of interpretation. De-hellenization is a new threshold of conscious activity that arises within phenomenological theology. However, some contemporary Western philosophical thinkers discount de-hellenization. And as a result many of believers miss the opportunity to engage the new threshold of theological inquiry that the Modernist movement has introduced.

In classical thinking, theoretical theological questions and answers have come to be determined within a fixed idea of nature and of being. As Henri Bergson (1944) understands them the forms or ideas of Plato or of Aristotle correspond to privileged or salient moments in the history of things, which in general, have been fixed by language. The notion of a contingent relationship, as anything but accidental, is impossible to conceive in classical philosophy. Moreover, the classical understanding of truth expressed in theoretical terms has become so fixed in a particular form of expression that, in the popular mind, that particular form is perceived to be as valid as the truth. Philosophers and theologians not aware of this aberration, in which the means have become equivalent to the ends, as it were, make interpretive mistakes. Such fixity of expression is not a problem in phenomenological understanding. In phenomenological understanding concepts have no independent existence apart from the conscious ness of the individual and thus there is no opportunity for them to become fixed. The fixed expression of truth does, however, remain a problem for scholastic philosophers and theologians. This problem is not reserved to the discipline of philosophy. This same problem of fixed expression has developed in the scientific disciplines and is easily demonstrated in psychology. The new threshold of understanding presented within phenomenological theology describes a relational and dynamic conception of truth that has replaced the fixed idea of truth.

A critical interpretation of history shows that philosophical schools of thought are related and do not come into being independently of each other. Phenomenological thought, as a description of a dynamic and relational conception of truth, in contrast to the scholastic static conception of truth, understands existence as becoming and unity as relational. These dynamic notions of becoming and unity, theologically understood, are rooted in the philosophy of Modernism. But, as well, these notions of becoming and unity are recognized in poetry. Thus, within a phenomenological perspective, they may be philosophically or poetically understood. Each is a legitimate mode, though different, of the interpretation of human experience. Since phenomenological theology is a kind of poetry, a pre-reflective understanding, I consider below the notion of poetic thresholds of phenomenological theological inquiry.

Poetic Thresholds of Phenomenological Theistic Theological Inquiry

Theistic theologians are continually searching for new and meaningful ways to understand their experience of God. Medieval clerics interpreted their experience within theoretical formulae. By not employing theoretical formulae, a poet's interpretation is free from the idealism of classical philosophy. Some contemporary theologians recognize the new language of phenomenological philosophy and theology as poetry, not prose. They insist that there are no hidden meanings contained in, or to be subsequently disclosed in, a phenomenological theological language. There is only an expression of the subject's intentional meaning. The contemporary theologian, J. Morreall (1983) writes:

> My conclusions regarding various appeals to hidden meaning for theological language, then, are negative. Our words are based on our intentions, and so if theological language is possible then theological intentions must be possible. We should not spend our time trying to appeal to hidden meanings for theological language.

Rather than disclose hidden meanings, as in an allegorical approach, phenomenological theistic theological language intentionally attributes religious meaning to phenomena, thus freeing human understanding from the limitations of allegory. Phenomenological theistic theology is original theology in that the phenomenological method presents a new threshold of consciousness for theological inquiry. Philosophers and theologians may undertake such inquiry but whether or not the phenomenologists of religion have grasped what is revealed by these methods is dubitable. Classical theology, unlike poetry or phenomenological theology, is a deductive science that uses the revealed propositions within sacred scripture as premises. Historically, this deductive type of science appealed to the Western mind and has made classical terms of reference and understanding normative for Western theology until the present day.

I suggest phenomenological philosophical interpretation is an attempt to get inside the mind of the believer. This goal may in fact, be achieved by poets. In contemporary Western culture, poetic interpretation presents a counterbalance to scholastic understanding. Poetic interpretations do not conform to the reasoned order of deductive science. The poetic interpretation of religious experience is, in fact, similar in kind to the philosophical phenomenological understanding of religious experience that discloses a new awareness of relationships. To be fair, however, it must be remembered that phenomenological theistic theological inquiry incorporates insights from both rational and poetic thought.

The disclosures of phenomenological understanding are not uniform. These disclosures depend upon the subject's point of view. Thus, the variety of phenomenological disclosures introduces new thresholds to Western theology. All these new perspectives are rooted in an existential understanding. Thinkers like Friedrich Schleiermacher

(1768–1834) Albrecht Ritschl (1822–1889) and John Henry Newman (1801–1890) through their innovative contributions, have shaped the contemporary Western problematic of phenomenological theological understanding. Given that these authors have helped to introduce a phenomenological way of thinking into modern theistic theology they are pioneers in providing alternative interpretations to the dominant classical interpretive perspective of the West. They helped make clear that the Western classical perspective is decreasingly viable and useful since contemporary Western culture is no longer Hellenist. Many of us can attest from our experience that the current method of integrating our Greek conceptual heritage has failed to construct a future for belief that is adequate for the present time

Within contemporary thinking a renaissance is occurring, as it were, as the phenomenological method reveals new thresholds of understanding within Western culture. I suggest that critical theologians, both inside and outside the Roman Catholic Church, are hopeful that contemporary theistic theology is on the verge of another grand synthesis that might supplant Thomism. Such a grand synthesis would need to be contingent upon the abandonment of traditional theoretical understanding. There is sufficient academic evidence to suggest that in classical speculative theology and popular devotional theology, traditional interpretations are changing. Pluralism in theology has always been present in the church to some degree. Today, this pluralism is clearly evident given the absence of a universally acceptable philosophy to support theology. Many critical thinkers in the West perceive that institutions and customs are no longer given from on high, as it were, as once was the case. Historical, geographical and human agencies all play a part in shaping the cultural, social and intellectual environment of the contemporary life-world. Also, the number of theologians accepting that there is no someone, external to experience determining the affairs of this life, is increasing. The contemporary perception is that many factors work in conjunction with our own efforts. A way forward, I suggest, is through a poetical, or phenomenological philosophical, understanding as a basis to theistic theological inquiry.

VII PARTICULAR THRESHOLDS OF PHENOMENOLOGICAL INQUIRY

First Threshold: Universal Interpretation Shifts to Particular Understanding

In Western theological understanding, debate has moved from the question of the structure of religious language, an issue of classical interpretation, to the more radical question of religious language as a mode of meaningful discourse, an issue of phenomenological understanding, in which the interpreter is part of the interpretation. Phenomenological theologians look for new interpretations when seeking answers to their questions and consciously advance beyond the classical position. In part, theological interpretation is undergoing an *aggiornamento*, an up-dating and becoming disengaged from the Roman Imperial culture that no longer exists. In short, theological interpretation has entered new thresholds of interpretation. It is generally understood, particularly among Roman Catholics, that *aggiornamento* began with Pope John XXIII. However, Heinrich Ott (1967) writing from the perspective of ecumenical inquiry into the disclosure of the meaning of spiritual values, says:

> Again, although the Roman Catholic Church cannot alter the dogmas which it has defined in virtue of its teaching office, yet it in no way knows what future formulations will appear as a result of the process of understanding and interpretation. That someday a future pope will authoritatively interpret or reformulate one or another of the doctrinal teachings that have divided the churches, *e.g.*, the doctrine of papal infallibility, in

such a way that it could be acceptable to us Protestants, upon that rests a genuine ecumenical hope.

It is highly probable that for doctrinal teaching to be reformulated, a pope would need to abandon the classical interpretation in favour of a phenomenological interpretation. Pope John Paul II (1994) encouragingly seems to give approval to phenomenological inquiry within contemporary thought when he writes:

> In gaining some distance from positivistic convictions, contemporary thought has made notable advances toward the ever more complete discovery of man, recognizing among other things the value of metaphorical and symbolic language. Contemporary hermeneutics, examples of which are found in the work of Paul Ricoeur or, from a different perspective, in the work of Emmanuel Lévinas presents the truth about man and the world from new angles.

In the context of a deeper philosophical awareness a co-responsible and co-creative relationship is disclosed in a phenomenological understanding of the contemporary life-world. This is significant because as an individual I now may identify myself as a co-responsible and co-creative agent in a relationship with that which is divine. In a classical approach such an understanding of co-responsibility and co-creatorship is not tenable. Within a phenomenological approach it is tenable. In the classical approach Roman Catholic theologians hold that creatures reveal a God-directed orientation within the world. Also, many Roman Catholic theologians believe that humanity, like concrete things, possesses a nature heading toward a proper perfection of itself.

I suspect that many contemporary philosophers view the understanding of the co-creator relationship as being characteristic of a New Age consciousness. That is, they view it as somewhat heretical. However, the co-creator relationship is an evolution in philosophical methodology, resulting from the development of new phenomenological thresholds. The co-creator relationship does not occur simply to remove the academic boredom of classical thought. Rather, it results legitimately from a phenomenological theistic theological inquiry into new thresholds that seeks new meaning arising from the believer's experience. Evolution leads to a new kind of experience, not to a difference of degree in a present experience according to Henri Bergson (1944). Many contemporary Western-educated individuals understand themselves as faithful co-responsible agents and seek new thresholds for theological inquiry, which express their participatory role in the religious interpretation of their life-world. It must be recalled that classical theological understanding does not falsify interpretations rather it is inadequate for the contemporary interpretive task. A phenomenological interpretation of the Christian believer's experience of the holy or sacred reveals the meaningfulness of the *theologia crucis* (theology of the cross). However, this understanding of the holy or sacred, the *theologia crucis*, is not disclosed in the experience of the believer in Judaism or Islam.

The Christian's life-world amounts to the *theologia crucis*, that is, a world that embraces a theology of the cross, in which religious suffering must be engaged. The *theologia crucis* is a particular *locus* of phenomenological philosophical investigation. Undertaken in Modernity, the phenomenological philosophical investigation of the *theologia crucis* does not accept the criteria or standards supplied by another epoch. This is so since Modernity creates its norms out of itself. In an existential and phenomenological understanding of the *theologia crucis*, theology becomes fundamentally an activity of deconstruction, construction and reconstruction, but not of proposition or exposition, as theology has been understood in the past. In contemporary theology, there is still no universal hermeneutic, no clear method, no set of rules to secure a definite interpretation and understanding of religious experience. However, there is a relational approach to religious experience that suggests a particular threshold of participation and interpretation for the individual believer.

Second Threshold: Classical Knowledge Shifts to Phenomenological Knowledge

In this short section I consider the philosophical shift in epistemological thinking from a classical to a phenomenological way of thinking. When philosophers attend to their proper role, that is, asking questions that no science or technology can answer on their behalf, they may become less certain but more flexible so that theology can utilize their support. Within this philosophical shift, from a static (classical) knowledge to a participatory (phenomenological) knowledge, subjectivism is not to be confused with subjectivity. Subjectivism and its counterpart, objectivism, denote specific doctrines or systems of knowledge, whereas subjectivity and its counterpart, objectivity, are notions connoting a phenomenological and relational view of the life-world. More will be said about this distinction below.

Theologians interpret their experience of the life-world according to the epistemological norms of their period. Thomas Aquinas, whose interpretation was greatly influenced by Aristotle, teaches that human knowledge comes through one's innate capacity to know, as well as, through one's experience. In the table below I juxtapose particular religious concepts that illustrate the difference between classical understanding and phenomenological understanding within a theistic theological understanding. The theistic theological concept is listed in the centre of the table with the contrasting understandings on the side.

Fig.1 <u>Contrasted understandings</u>

CLASSICAL UNDERSTANDING	THEISTIC THEOLOGICAL CONCEPT	PHENOMENOLOGICAL UNDERSTANDING
In the beginning	Creator	Co-creator
Ransom for sin	Redemption	A way travelled
Grace	New creation	Indwelling person
Revelation	Hierarchical church	Spirit-filled people
Heaven	Salvation	Communion with humanity
Morality/Ethics	Legal norms	Personal values

In classical theological thinking, characteristics modeled on anthropomorphic ideas are predicated of that which is divine. Further, these predicates are often interpreted as real, not symbolic, in the public mind and as constituting God *in se* (in himself). That divinity is believed to be an "Other," or is understood as "Other," does not reveal any characteristic of the divine nature. Nor does it reveal whether God or gods exist. In contrast to classical thought, phenomenological thought does not inquire into objective reality. It inquires into subjective reality. That is, phenomenological thinking inquires into noetic reality that originates in the mind (from the Greek: *nous* – mind), or, stated alternatively into consciousness. Classical philosophy posits that a true, absolute being, one who is all-powerful, all-knowing and transcendent, personally exists over and above the temporal world, imparting knowledge to the knower. In classical philosophy beings lack the potential for any essential development or true evolution.

Beings undergo change through accidents in classical philosophy. This contrasts with phenomenological philosophy in which an evolutionary understanding of the activity of beings occurs. In phenomenological philosophy relationships are socially intended or constructed rather than conceived intellectually, that is, in theory. To my mind, in the West, phenomenological philosophy has been gaining credibility since the beginning of the Reformation.

A relational epistemology reflects a phenomenological understanding of social and cultural symbols that engage the thinker in a relationship. The thinker is convinced of the social and cultural reality indicated by the symbol. Since phenomenological interpretation is symbolically, that is, subjectively constructed, I experience my existence in terms of these symbolic constructions. Social symbols require an active context or they cannot become reflective of my experience. That is, they have no meaning outside my human activity. In contrast, signs admit no active social nuance in my experience. By its presence a sign has static meaning outside my subjectivity. Thus, by virtue of its existence a "stop sign," or a "no entry" sign, signifies an objectively socially agreed-upon significance regardless of location or context. Thus, it is clear that symbols, not signs, present themselves as thresholds for participatory knowledge and phenomenological interpretation. These thresholds for participatory knowledge are susceptible to an intersubjective agreement among subjects. In short, the ideological "sign" has shifts to the phenomenological "symbol."

Third Threshold: Idealistic Language and Interpretation Shifts to Participatory/poetic Language and Interpretation

Theological language is convictional language of a special type, but it is not necessarily confessional language. That is to say, convictional language expresses a firm belief, whereas confessional language acknowledges belief, firm or otherwise. To my mind, convictional language is unique due to its idealistic, not descriptive, character. Convictional language is based on one's rational understanding. Theological confessional language, however, is a deeper conscious statement of what the believer actually believes, reason notwithstanding. However, theological language, either convictional or confessional, defies conventional semantics and is self-consciously revelatory (Raschke, 1979). I suggest, then, that understanding theistic theological language, convictional or confessional, phenomenologically, shifts the threshold of interpretation from idealistic language to participatory language, based on relationships. Thus, from a phenomenological point of view, Bishop Berkley's (1685–1753) observation *esse est percipi*, that is, being is perception, is better rendered *esse est referri*, being is relational (Dewart, 1989). *Esse est referri* is preferred since phenomenological understanding involves a self-conscious relationship which discloses an understanding of that which is meaningful in a relationship.

Phenomenological theistic understanding is an artistic, or poetic, activity, which must be interpreted existentially since it is the form and the meaning of human life that is being constructed and reconstructed in phenomenological philosophy. Phenomenological theistic understanding, or its corollary, poetic understanding, as a new threshold is a participatory form of understanding. Michael Murray (1975) writes of articulates phenomenological participation in artistic interpretation this way:

> Receiving the truth as an event that casts me in a new situation is the work of interpretation. In interpretation we attempt to articulate this experience with its source in the work of art; to place the self in a position to be claimed by the work, to hear what it says, to enter the realm of its sway.

Theistic phenomenological participation is similar to the activity of the artist, or poet, and is not to be understood merely scientifically. Thus, theistic artistry is not to be understood as re-producing or re-presenting something. Rather, it is to be understood as expressive of an original encounter in a new threshold open to an intersubjective relationship. So, in liturgical theological interpretation, original experience is given a new expression in such a way that I, as a subject, not only know the content of the original experience but, will be able to have my own experience of the original. That is to say, I participate in it. A phenomenological interpretation of, or participation in, my life-world occurs through poetry, drama, and literature. Since individual poetic constructions are presented through social structures particular to a given culture, poetry is capable, up to a point, of being embraced by the whole community within that culture. However, no artistic construction originating in one culture seems capable of translation to another culture without serious adaptation by, or alteration to, the receiving culture. In short, there are no universal poetic or phenomenological constructions, only particular poetic, or phenomenological constructions. Phenomenological construction requires a shift to a new threshold of consciousness by each individual in each culture. The foregoing notwithstanding, many Western thinkers hold poetry and classical philosophy to be mutually exclusive. It is well known among professional philosophers that Aristotle believed poetry to be for one's delight and not for the critical examination of life.

Despite the reservations about a phenomenological philosophy the Second Vatican Council did tolerate a phenomenological and existential understanding of the social, or pastoral, context. In giving a qualified approval to a phenomenological approach, the Council's pastoral constitution, *Gaudium et Spes,* (Art 62) acknowledges that the recent studies and findings of science, history, and philosophy do raise new questions which influence life and demand new theological investigations. Some Catholic theologians have maintained that, by the end of its deliberations, Vatican II did subscribe to phenomenology as its dominant method of understanding. Other Catholic theologians make a stronger statement in that the Council itself was self-consciously an exercise in the phenomenological method of interpreting church doctrine. A noted phenomenologist, John Kobler (2000), basing his observations on the Council's self-conscious initiative, offers phenomenological arguments in lieu of the traditional Roman Catholic scholastic perspective. However, in what seems to be a reactionary move, John Paul II (1993) writes in *Veritatis Splendor* (Art 4) that:

> in particular, note should be taken on the *lack of harmony between the traditional response of the Church and certain theological positions*...these being left to the judgment of the individual subjective conscience or to the diversity of social and cultural contexts [John Paul's italics].

It appears that John Paul's encyclical cautions against the phenomenological method of interpreting the experience of the individual believer. However, in my reading of the Encyclical, it is individualism, not individuality, to which he is opposed in whatever philosophical or social context it appears. Classical Roman Catholic theology in its contemporary form, known as Neo-Thomism, often fails to satisfy intellectual curiosity. As a result of this dissatisfaction a new renaissance seems to be occurring in Western theological thinking in which phenomenological theology is beginning to replace classical theology.[2]

---

2 I concluded that phenomenological philosophy is replacing scholastic philosophy in liturgical understanding in my D.Th. thesis, University of South Africa (1996), entitled "A Phenomenological Understanding of Certain Liturgical Texts: The Anglican Collects for Advent and the Roman Catholic Collects for Lent."

An insight, peculiar to the phenomenological method, is that knowledge arises within a personal and conscious act. Thus, in phenomenological understanding to know is to be conscious. But this innovative process of phenomenologically conscious inquiry into new thresholds of understanding does not occur without resistance. Concerning the phenomenological thresholds of theistic theological inquiry there are competing philosophies, which promote opposing philosophical positions. One such opposing intention is the return to the classical thought of Neo-scholasticism.

VIII PHENOMENOLOGY AND THE CATHOLICITY OF VATICAN II: A BROAD CRITICISM

Phenomenological Understanding of the Church as Theological Mystery

In this book I distinguish between speculative language and qualitative language. Speculative language belongs to classical philosophy, whereas qualitative language belongs to phenomenological philosophy. The suffixes "-ism" and "-ity" reflect this distinction. Funk and Wagnall's *Canadian College Dictionary* defines "-ism" as a suffix attached to nouns to mean "a distinctive theory, doctrine, or system: usually used disparagingly;" and "-ity" is a suffix attached to nouns to mean a "state, condition, or quality." The following pairs of terms, often used in discussions in philosophy and theology illustrate this distinction: spiritualism vs. spirituality, materialism vs. materiality, personalism vs. personality, humanism vs. humanity, nationalism vs. nationality, historicism vs. historicity, Catholicism vs. Catholicity, individualism vs. individuality, modernism vs. modernity, dualism vs. duality, rationalism vs. rationality, moralism vs. morality, Deism vs. Deity. Words ending in "-ity" reflect a phenomenological language, whereas words ending in "-ism" reflect a speculative philosophical language.

This short book, as noted earlier, is a product of my reflection. It is not a history of religious thought. Nor is it written in the form of a traditional catechism founded on the school of scholastic theology. Rather, it is a philosophical reflection intended to reconstruct pre-Vatican II theological ideas in light of contemporary philosophical understanding.

Although I examine issues from a Western Catholic philosophical point of view, my observations may be applied, *inter alia*, to the entire Western Christian social and pastoral tradition. My examination is undertaken from within the collective body of believers, that is, the Church. The Church must be the *locus* of my study since there is no divine guarantee for isolated inquiry in the Christian philosophical tradition. In my inquiry, I do accept that there are limits to "Catholicism," the traditional concept, but what of "Catholicity," the contemporary notion? To my mind, Catholicism is limited by scholastic philosophy, whereas Catholicity is free from scholastic constraints.

The exercise of private judgment, which distinguished Protestant from Catholic theologians in Pre-Vatican II times, no longer accurately characterizes this division. In fact, in the contemporary context both Protestants and Catholics exercise private judgment. A convert to Roman Catholicism in the Victorian era, George Tyrrell noted that the Protestant believer accepts scripture as functioning as the supreme rule, whereas, the Catholic believer accepts the Church as functioning as the supreme rule. What unites their behaviour is that both interpret these rules through an exercise of private judgment. It is to charismatic Christianity, as revealed in the New Testament and, not to the ecclesiastical institution of the time, that the Protestant believer looks for the light of Christ. The Catholic believer, however, looks to a spirit-guided ecclesiastical institution, not to charismatic Christianity. Charismatic Christianity, of the type recorded in the New Testament, reflects a period of historical inspiration and enchantment. As long as conditions for inspiration and enchantment continued, as it is argued, there was no need for a formal organization that might hinder, as opposed to enable, the action of the spirit. A critical reading of the history of theology shows that scientific and historical advancement became a problem, not for the Church as is popularly supposed, but for the philosophy and the theology giving expression to the Church's experience. Scientific and historical advancement is primarily an epistemological problem for philosophical and theological interpretation and only secondarily a problem of faith for the historical church, or, rather the *ecclesia*. More is said about this distinction below.

Existential philosophy, which has gained influence within Catholic philosophy since the Second Vatican Council, encourages historical criticism. The scriptures, as documents of revelation, are susceptible to the laws of textual criticism as is any historical document. In the case of the scriptures, textual criticism discloses the literary customs of the era in which they were written. In this regard, George Tyrrell (1910) writes:

> We do not ask if Socrates really said what Plato puts into his mouth; but we may rationally ask: 'Is Plato's Socrates the true Socrates? Similarly may we not perhaps be justified in asking: Did Christ do or say all that the Fourth Gospel ascribes to him?' but only in asking: 'Is the Johannine Christ the true Christ a true resetting and idealisation of Christ.'

The scriptures were not written as chronological history and cannot be used as any sort of "proof-text" to establish Jesus' divinity. In light of modern scriptural studies since 1900, I conclude, along with George Tyrrell, that the Christian scriptures are:

> an insufficient basis for the scientific establishment of a single clear fulfilment of prophecy...[and] the New Testament has been both consciously and unconsciously doctored into an agreement with prophecy so as to bring home to the Jews an *ad hominem* argument for Christ's Messiahship (Sagovsky, 1990).

Further, with reference to the Council of Florence (1431-1438), George Tyrrell noted that since then all that was taught about dogmas, sacraments and Church government from the Roman Catholic point of view was accepted as fully known to Peter and his successors. This pre-Vatican II view, which he criticized, is no longer tenable given the contemporary and ecumenical theological climate. I reject the theological understanding that supported the Council of Florence and rely on the theological insights, characteristic of George Tyrrell, in examining of the move from a scholastic to a phenomenological philosophical understanding. In short, in this book I am examining the move towards Catholicity and, away from Catholicism, in the theological understanding after Vatican II.

It was evident to George Tyrrell that the historical criticism of the late 1800's revealed that ecclesiastical government had developed *de facto* from a loose federation of organized democratic communities into the highly centralized and hierarchical ecclesiastical structure in which all the teaching authority was being invested in the pope. It appeared that the teaching authority would be taken away from the ecumenical councils and episcopate in which it then resided. A phenomenological philosophical interpretation of the Church's teaching authority is not the ossified epistemology that scholasticism had become in the theological schools of Tyrrell's day. He observed that the schoolmen equated faith with theological orthodoxy and they assumed that Christ's mission was primarily theological. These schoolmen argued that the Church must necessarily possess the same authority, which Christ possessed in settling doubts about his teaching and miracles on earth. In default of biblical inspiration, such a view of the Church's authority as purported by the schoolmen can only be held through a combination of a philosophical and theological dialectic, (dare I say rhetoric?), and papal infallibility. According to Tyrrell, in the Johannine and Pauline writings the first beginnings of philosophic reflection on the teaching of Christ are clearly evident. However, the Johannine and Pauline reflection and teaching was proper to their culture, and not to that of the Western scholastic tradition, nor to our contemporary culture.

The Catholic theological system, in principle, is as old as the first epistle of St Clement, (circa 75–110), in which the Church is conceived as a divine institution. It is conceived as a corporation possessing officers whose duty is independent of their personal gifts and determined solely by official position. In this regard they are analogous to officers of the state.

> That the institutional form was absolutely necessary for the saving of Christianity from speedy disintegration no one will deny; but it is in asserting the Divine origin of the Ecclesiastical Polity and of the *Civitas Dei* that Catholicism is at one with St Clement, and at variance with the critics (Tyrrell, 1910).

What have the contemporary critics to say about Catholicity, not Catholicism, and the institutional form, I ask? Given my understanding from the textual criticism of scripture, I suggest that the Christ would never contemplate grace attaching to any form of government, ecclesiastical or state, as opposed to the person. It is clear that the apostles believed in the end of the world within their lifetime and made no provision for an institutional future as we know it and live in it today.

The spirit that animates the Church today animated the Christ. To my mind, this same spirit reveals an understanding of Catholicity, not Catholicism within the Church today. As Tyrrell expressed it: Christ and the Church are different and complementary organs of the spirit's own expression adapted to different phases of the same movement (Tyrrell, 1910). I suggest that Tyrrell's thinking supports the understanding of Catholicity, rather than that of Catholicism, even though he writes with the classical vocabulary of Catholicism. The ecclesiastical institution is designed to perpetuate and promote, among the uninspired millions of believers, the conceptions and ideals revealed by the perceived founder of the Christian movement, that is, Jesus of Nazareth. According to the Church's teaching authority the institution embodies only a variation of the original revelation and never creates a new revelation. This is a political presumption of expediency rather than a philosophical insight of the Western academic tradition. A challenging insight within contemporary theology is the notion of *homo faber* vs. that of *homo creator*. If normative revelation ceased with the death of the last apostle, how Catholicity differs from Catholicism becomes a significant question. Catholicity is primarily a way or manner of life based on Jesus of Nazareth that has been committed to the guardianship of the Church, rather than a body of doctrine imparted to the Church about Jesus of Nazareth. In short, the spirit of the Christ, not Christology, has been revealed to the Church. Thus, to my mind, the spirit of Christ is authentically interpreted phenomenologically in the contemporary ecclesial community.

The Spirit of the Christ appropriates from a multitude of beliefs, theological, ethical, and historical, those that are most suitable for its own embodiment and adapts them to its present purposes. The Spirit of the Christ uses the knowledge at hand to develop public doctrine based on a human understanding. To this end, then, the true teacher in the Church is the Spirit of the Christ, or the Holy Spirit, acting immediately in and through the whole body of the faithful both lay and ordained. In concert with the Spirit of the Christ, the teaching activity of the episcopate consists in dispensing to and, in gathering from, all the faithful. In dispensing to and in gathering from all, the Magisterium acts with the authority of and, in the name of, the whole ecclesial community.

Regarding the Thomistic approach to theology, which is characteristic of traditional and hierarchical Christianity, Aquinas did leave a particular foundation to posterity. He left his theological *Summa* but he did not leave his liberal theological spirit, that is, his gifted insight into what was going on in the minds of those around him. His liberal theological spirit, in appropriating the methods of criticism current in his day, seems to be lost to us. A true theologian, such as Thomas, is one who speaks from an inward spirit and is, in fact, a rarity. Any priest, or minister, can instruct us and tell us what the Church teaches and believes. In our day the sense of official instruction, which continues to dominate the institutional Church and, threatens the charismatic spirit of theology. History and experience show that the spirit of Christ does work outside the official Church. Thus, one may be historically severed from the official Constantinian Church, but not the Church of Christ, which subsists in the Catholic Church. A phenomenological understanding of Catholicity, or the Spirit of Christ, discloses the theological significance of what Vatican II intended when it affirmed that the Church of Christ subsists in the Catholic Church (*Lumen Gentiuim*, para. 8).

Owing to the philosophical circumstances of our time, that is, the evolutionary stage of philosophy in which we find ourselves, I examine the Church's situation and mission in light of the fact that a Hellenized philosophy no longer satisfactorily meets the needs of Christ's faithful. As a member of Christ's faithful, I live in a new age of history as societal and cultural change continues throughout the entire world. Such societal and cultural change has theological implications for me as one of Christ's faithful. My faith tells me that I am to be saved as an individual person and that human society is to be renewed within this same salvific process. The divine life in me is shared within the Church, that is, Christ's other faithful members and, in turn, the Church shares it with humanity. Humanity searches for a better world but often without seeking a better philosophical explanation of its experience than the one it has inherited. From my experience, I know that an evolutionary concept of nature is in the process of replacing the classical static concept of nature. This presents new problems for philosophy and theology, which call for a new analysis. The classical and historical solutions must be replaced by phenomenological philosophical solutions. Henri Bergson's (1944) insightful notion is at work here. Evolution renders asunder, in order to develop them to the end those elements, which at their origin, interpenetrated each other.

Within human society there is a sense that human beings are destined for a higher life. However, that higher life originates in this world. Humans are at the centre and summit of that life which extends beyond the incarnated boundaries of human misery, that is, to a transcendental life. Out of the history of Israel, and here I mean the history that is intended by the German, *heilige geschichte*, or salvation history, has come the realization of the Church as theological mystery. In this incarnated life the church grows into maturity and longs for a completed kingdom within the mystery of the Incarnation of Jesus of Nazareth. In this incarnated life, through the sacraments, the faithful are united to Christ within the Church. Christ established his community as a society of faith, hope and charity and as an existential community on earth. He did so without any historical politically governing structure. Therein is the theological mystery. The phenomenological body of Christ and the salvific existential community together constitute the mystery of the Church as one organic community. Theologians today, then, must work with the methods of philosophical science to establish the credibility of this community for the contemporary generation. In establishing this credibility for the contemporary generation a freedom of philosophical inquiry into the theological mystery of the Church is needed to accomplish this task.

Phenomenological Theology and the People of God: The Ecclesia

The Church, or better, the *ecclesia*, is composed of individuals constituting a relational bond among all the faithful. This bond reflects the divine life in the world. For the Christian, it is the spirit of the risen Christ who constitutes this bond and calls all the faithful to him forming a new people of God, not according to the flesh, but according to the Spirit (1 Cor. 11:25). "According to the flesh" signifies the historically constituted People of God, whereas "according to the spirit" signifies the phenomenologically constituted People of God. In other words, the *ecclesia* has evolved, and is evolving from an existential historical entity to an existential phenomenological entity. The existential mission of the *ecclesia* is primarily salvific, and only secondarily, political, economic or social. The salvific mission of the *ecclesia* is not connected to any one particular culture or philosophical system. It transcends history by its phenomenological constitution, yet is mysteriously incarnated in history.

> By its nature and mission the church is universal in that it is not committed to any one culture or to any political, economic or social system. Hence, it can be a very close bond between the communities of peoples and nations, provided they trust the church and guarantee its true freedom to carry out its mission (Flannery, 1996).

In the phenomenological understanding of the nature of the *ecclesia*, the priesthood of the faithful and the hierarchical priesthood are organically related. However, these priestly offices differ ontologically and each is a separate phenomenon. They constitute an organic, not mechanical, unified phenomenological entity. Collectively, all Christ's faithful, lay and ordained constitute a universal entity when confessing matters of faith and morals. This confession is a consensus, or *sensus fidelium*, which originates in and, is maintained by, the phenomenologically understood presence of the spirit. Phenomenologically understood, then, Christ's faithful as the People of God, the *ecclesia*, transcend the historical Constantinian Christian People of God, that is, the ecclesiastical, not ecclesial, community. Constantine, it will be remembered, was the Roman Emperor, whose Edit of Milan (313) gave legal status to the Christians of the Empire.

Within the course of my reflections, major cultural changes have caused me to conceive of a new age in human history and in which I recognized myself as an agent of some these same cultural changes that affect my understanding of the *ecclesia*. The realization of such reflections remains problematic after Vatican II, particularly for the Catholic faithful, who continue to discern the presence of God in the changes brought about by *ressourcement* and *aggiornamento*. [3] To my mind, one such problem remains the incorporation of the individual into the phenomenological *ecclesia vis à vis* the incorporation of the individual into the visible ecclesiastical corporation. This was a problem for the theologians of Vatican II, which they addressed to varying degrees of satisfaction. The Council has maintained that the individual person who does not persevere in charity is not saved, even though incorporated into the church. Such people remain indeed in the bosom of the church, but only 'bodily' not 'in their hearts' (*L.G.* para. 14. Flannery, 1996).

In most hierarchical churches it is believed that the teaching of the bishops, under the inspiration of the spirit, governs Christ's faithful. This teaching reflects a three-fold relationship among the bishop, priest and deacon within God's flock committed to them by Christ. Catholicism is the most readily and popular example available of this belief as a religious corporation. The theologians subscribing to the

---

3 *Ressourcement*: a return to the sources, which implies less centralization by Rome; *aggiornamento*: the process of bringing an institution or organization up to date. Catholic theologians consider these as opposing terms.

Catholicity of the *ecclesia* understand that bishops alone are successors to the pastoral responsibilities given to the apostles. However, they share in this responsibility through delegation to the priest and deacon in a collegiate structure more deeply understood phenomenologically than in a Hellenized fashion. Given an awareness of New Testament textual criticism contemporary Bishops are motivated to present Christ's teachings in a manner relevant to the needs of the times. Hierarchically constituted churches, phenomenologically understood enjoy an organic relationship among themselves, each with its own liturgical, spiritual and theological patrimony. Thus, in this understanding, when the Roman Pontiff makes infallible pronouncements it is not as a private person, but as one in whom the infallibility of the *ecclesia* resides in a collegial manner. Thus, such pronouncements present the deposit of the faith such that no new public revelation, or addition to revelation, is required for salvation.

Many lay individuals require a deeper knowledge of revelation and a deeper wisdom than is currently possessed in order to assist the *ecclesia* in the circumstances of our day. Like the hierarchy, the laity has its role to play in interpreting revelation. The laity are related to the hierarchy in an organic expression of the *ecclesia* and equally they constitute Christ's faithful. All Christ's faithful are called to holiness and are partakers in the divine presence. The laity, which includes those who are in a religious, or vowed, state of life, constitute a portion of the *ecclesia* and are to be distinguished from the hierarchy.

Thinking, about religion whether by hierarchy or laity, and as guided by God's presence, I call theology. As one of the new People of God my theistic theology presupposes that I recognize my acquired desire, a philosophical desire, for religious understanding as a conscious movement-toward-God. In fact, I am a being destined-for-God. In this understanding my philosophical attitude, as pre-requisite, leads me to self-discovery, to seeing for myself and to doing for myself. Since I undertake my self-discovery within a believing community I clarify my particular experience through philosophical intersubjectivity as a theologian. Such intersubjectivity discloses that God is moving toward the subject, me, as well as, other faithful subjects.

As a theologian I can never complete the interpretive task, which engages me. But, I need to embrace a philosophy that will be suitable to giving theological expression to the true meaning of God's revelation to the *ecclesia*. The most appropriate philosophy, for me, as I try to explicate what is known implicitly about God and revelation through my lived experience, is existential phenomenology. I therefore must remain in close contact with the hopes and anxieties of my own time. Only in such a relationship can Christian revelation speak to me in a truly meaningful way. Phenomenology makes it possible for me to reflect upon myself, and revelation in a manner that is unthinkable and not possible, within scholasticism. With this in mind, there is only one activity, which affects me and allows me to realize the true meaning of God's influence on me. That activity is called love. Love allows for intersubjectivity. In short, love permits the other to be subject for me. In other words, the other cannot be an object if loved by me. Thus, it can be easily understood that a phenomenological understanding of love has a greater usefulness for the theology than a philosophy of reason. A loving encounter of two human subjects effects a participation in philosophical transcendental reality. When God is the other, the participation is in the fullness of theological transcendental reality. The subject, which I am, is the result of the divine creative love affecting in me a natural desire to see God. My thinking here reflects that of St Augustine. For you have made us for yourself and our heart is restless until its rests in you. [4] Nor can I

---

4 *Confessions*, Book I: I.1.

initiate this intersubjective relationship with God. I can only respond to God's existential invitation to me. Such is the deeper wisdom arising out of revelation with which the believing laity must assist the *ecclesia* in the circumstances of our day.

The Development of my Christian Understanding

Ultimately, I may have to accept divergent conceptualizations of God and live accordingly. That is, I must live in God's presence as co-creator. This will involve, on my part, the development of alternative philosophical understanding to my present philosophical understanding. One such alternative philosophical understanding is that my self-fulfillment is intrinsically connected to my self-realization. That is to say, my self-fulfillment and self-realization are no longer connected to an ideological understanding that is distinct from me. This is the philosophical position that I have abandoned. Rather, what I make myself to be, my self-realization, places me in a unique existential relationship to God, thus affecting my self-fulfillment in God's presence. My purposiveness is my intention determined internally, it is not purpose, which is my intention as acquired externally. My purposiveness arises in my seeking creatively to be. My self-creation takes place in the presence of God, which is God's self-communication to me. It is a given, then, that what I make of myself, does make a real difference in my moral relationship with God.

Among the first things I must abandon philosophically is that the illusion does not exist. That is, it is an illusion to believe that reality is properly, necessarily and exclusively conceivable as being. Unless I accept this I cannot conceive reality at all. That is the illusion. In short, reality is not being. As a classically thinking Christian I am able to equate intelligibility and necessity only as long as I reject belief in evolution.

Intelligibility and necessity require the adoption of a non-evolutionary Hellenic philosophical viewpoint. My proper development of theism, then, given my everyday experience requires dehellenization of dogma and doctrine. Phenomenological dehellenization of understanding requires that the Christian doctrine of God be philosophically reformulated. Thus, dehellenization is my conscious reformulation of the inherited doctrine, which I currently require for the future of my belief. In other words, as a positive concept, dehellenization means my conscious creation of the future of my belief. My creation of the future of my belief implies that my Christian theistic theology has become conscious and that its traditional form has evolved. Further, my theistic theology continues to evolve at an ever more sophisticated level of experience and cultural interpretation. Thus, in a world come of age, my theism comes of age.

For the anti-theist God is thinkable because of a denied relationship. For the a-theist God is not thinkable because no relationship obtains between the two. On this point, Christianity, to my knowledge, is the only religion to have generated atheism within itself. Atheism, as a cultural phenomenon, is solely indigenous to Christian societies. That is, none but the Christian cultures have ever generated atheism, and I find it difficult to think that other cultures could ever do so – unless infected by Western philosophy. My faith is a commitment of my existential self to reality, not being, as disclosed in my lived relational experience. Such faith is the existential response of my self to the openness of a transcendent reality to which I am related within my conscious experience. I cannot believe in God once-for-all any more than, I can exist once-for-all. I cannot, without committing idolatry, believe in anything or anyone else in the same way in which I believe in God.

A *post-facto* theological understanding is a property of my human nature. That is, I understand upon reflection. I do not need to be a Christian to do this. However, it is no coincidence that I reached this reflective understanding concerning myself at the same time that I reached the awareness of my historicity and my conscious nature. The fact is that I am aware that I develop historically as a Christian and, that I interpret my experience within a Christian consciousness. That is, my belief and consciousness are uniquely Christian. Auguste Sabatier's (2003) view reflects my understanding when he notes that the Christian consciousness is not merely an accidental form or part of the general religious consciousness of humanity, it is a necessary and dominant part of it, to which all the others tend as to their ideal, and in which alone they find their explanation and perfecting. My conscious life is distinguished from an animal's conscious life in a way more significant than in the classical philosophical tradition, which conceives humans as merely thinking animals. That humans are merely thinking animals is a legacy of the early Greek philosophical tradition. In my recent philosophical thinking I have concluded that my human conscious life exhibits a peculiar characteristic that animals do not appear to share. That is, I am a being who is consciously present to myself. Both, animals and I "know" but the true difference is not one of a higher degree of knowledge on my part. The true difference is reflective thinking, which transcends the order of the classical understanding of knowledge. To my mind, this means that I can know not only existential beings, but also dynamic being and, not only being-as-other, but also being-in-itself. In short, I can know what it means to be, or not to be, in a sense greater than Shakespeare was able to comprehend.

Conventional Christian theistic theological development takes the form of an increase in philosophical data. However, conventional theistic theological development increases with data, which is quantitative and to be contrasted with theological development that is the result of a deepening in consciousness, which is qualitative. A deepening in my qualitative theistic theological development occurs as I become more deeply conscious of that which I already was aware, that is, of that of which I was already originally conscious. By that I mean that in deepening my consciousness I realize, that is, make truly real, that which had been in my understanding and in my consciousness all the time. My qualitative experience has presented to me that which is truly real. Indeed, I have already understood, but now I understand all over again in a new light, that is, with a sharper, clearer, and deepened meaning. But, this new meaning I have acquired is not a substitute for the earlier one. This new meaning is possible only insofar as it emerges from the earlier one, which it incorporates and thus creates a "fuller" and "richer" experience for me. In Western traditional understanding to know a thing more thoroughly often means to know more things about the same thing. This is not so in phenomenological understanding. This deepening of consciousness, or realization of a clearer meaning, presupposes a genuine but underdeveloped earlier consciousness. Thus, any new meaning can only grow out of and be truly meaningful in relation to my former, but underdeveloped, consciousness. There are theological implications to this understanding. The absence of public revelation after the close of the New Testament era means that Christianity cannot teach any previously unknown truths. The Trinity and Incarnation were revealed and taught, albeit in an incomplete manner, through Judaism to Christianity. Once this is understood by the Christian faithful, revelation can only deepen the understanding of the truths of faith already present to the believer.

My conscious life is not constituted by my mind achieving existential union with a reality from which it was originally separated. Rather, my conscious life is constituted by my mind achieving self-differentiation out of reality within which it was originally un-differentiated. In other words, my conscious life and my existential unity with reality are as equi-primordial. Thus, my consciousness is a process whereby my coming-into-being emerges through self-awareness. Thus, consciousness is not my being coming into existence, but consciousness is the coming-into-being of my unique identity. There is, then, no real difference in me between consciousness and self-consciousness.

In light of the foregoing understanding, I recognize that truth is not the adequacy of my understanding to an idea or ideal, but rather it is the adequacy of my conscious existence. The truth is what it is only because it is the result of the process of my conscious self-creation. Truth is the relation of my being and my becoming conceived as fidelity rather than as conformity. Conformity, classically understood, is my relation towards another, which is owing to another by reason of the other's nature. Fidelity, phenomenologically understood, is my relation towards another, which I owe to myself by reason of my nature. In other words, conformity, like union, obligates me from without. Fidelity, like unity, obligates me from within. My consciousness is not an independent private self-awareness, which is subsequently communicated through signs to other human beings. The private and personal nature of my consciousness is connected to my public and social existential presence. It is through the formation of concepts within my socio-historical life that my consciousness evolves. It is this conceptualization of my experience, which makes me conscious as well as makes me human. Concepts are the cultural forms of human experience, which reflect an ex-animal experience. The development of my consciousness requires the continuing development of concepts and conceptual systems. And to think in new concepts is to develop my original experience. Thus, I must develop culturally in order to exist.

Faith is a process by which I render myself present to that-in-which-I-believe. A concept is true if it describes the coming-into-being of my human experience. I may also say that a concept is true to the degree that it presents experience to my consciousness. In the theory of conceptualization I suggest my human knowledge is not the overcoming of an original separation in an existential context but, on the contrary, my knowledge is the self-differentiation of my consciousness from its original unity. The case is, then, that truthful concepts are not merely the subjective expression of an objective reality. Truthful concepts are the self-expression of my consciousness and are the means by which I objectify the world, and myself. Further, concepts are the means by which I objectify myself to another self, including God.

The Underdevelopment of my Christian Theism

Throughout the apostolic and patristic age Christianity grew within the gradual transformation of one cultural form to another. It was assumed that the truth of Christianity depended neither on the Hellenic culture, nor on the various local cultures in existence. Hellenism was the cultural form of the apostolic and patristic ecumenical world but it is not the cultural form of the world, as we know it today. However, in the West, it eventually became impossible to distinguish between the universalization of Christianity and the hellenization of Christianity. In short, Hellenism equaled Christianity. In contrast to the Hellenist culture, in the Hebraic culture, God is a transcendent presence. From a scholastic point of view, the theological conclusion is that Christ, as God, is essentially the redeemer of Israel. Within a Hebraic point of view, the conclusion is that the Word (*logos*) is the restorer of all things. In Hebraic culture God is a reality, other than being who is present to the creation of being. Yuval Lurie (2000) concludes that God is not a natural being and that the creation of nature is not a natural event, but a phenomenological narrative about the beginning of being and what God created ahead of all things, i.e., beings. Further, God is the reality, or agency, that makes beings to be what they are. Within this Hebraic philosophical perspective, persons cannot be the terminations, or necessary products of nature, as they are understood in Hellenist philosophy. Rather, the opposite is true, that is, nature is a termination or product of God's participatory agency. Persons construct their natures, as co-creators, in and through an incarnated existence within nature or within a termination of God's participatory agency.

Due to the influence of ancient Greek metaphysical thinking modern thinkers have accepted that in creatures there is a distinction to be made between essence and existence. Yet, in God there is no such distinction to be made between essence and existence. However, the creature/creator relationship that we accept today is not part of Greek metaphysics in its original and underdeveloped Hellenic philosophical form. The creature/creator relationship developed over a period of time and led to an insurmountable difference between the way God is *in se*, (in itself), and the way God is in our understanding. This distinction is a philosophical issue, not a theological issue. This philosophical distinction leads logically to either skepticism among unbelievers or to fideism among believers. The starting point of an adequate Christian philosophy for theistic believers is that it should begin with a consideration of the needs of the Christian faith, not the categories of Greek metaphysics. The obsolescence of Scholasticism has been brought about by the obsolescence of the Christian Hellenic cultural forms as foundational to modern thought. As a person, as a subject, I am a center of consciousness, not a static form, composed of substance and accidents. Consciousness is a phenomenological, not Hellenic, philosophical understanding. That is, I am that which can objectify my self to others and, as well, to myself. This reflexivity in thinking is a modern development. Thus, as my consciousness continues to develop beyond that of the Middle Ages, the usefulness of Scholasticism continues to wane.

Contemporary belief must bear directly upon the reality of God, not upon words or upon concepts about God. This follows upon the belief that God is immediately revealed. Words about God or concepts that mediate God's presence are not immediately revealed. For many, to believe in a concept of God is to believe in that to which they have become cognitively related. This, in effect, is St Thomas's understanding. It is the scholastic position in which consciousness bears directly upon a being that is conceptual. In Thomas's understanding conscious knowledge does not result from an intentional unity, (a psychological reality), of knower and known, subject and object but, rather, an intentional union, (an epistemological reality), of rational concepts that constitute knowledge according to classical philosophical understanding. In phenomenological philosophy the contingency of creatures is not to be conceived as an epistemological distinction between essence and existence, as if essence and existence existed in isolation from each other. Rather, the contingency of creatures is that quality of their non-separable character which consists in their differentiation, not separation, from their Creator. Thus, my personal contingency means that in order to be conscious of whom I am I must co-create myself with God's assistance. Yet, today, this notion of co-creation, as in the case of many, remains underdeveloped with respect to my Christian theism.

Two phenomenological philosophical thinkers, Gabriel Marcel (1889–1973) and Nicolas Berdyaev (1874–1948), do not conceive of any reality that is polarized in terms of existence and essence. They are concerned with being in its existential immediacy. They avoid every *a priori* construction as required by scholastic philosophy to distinguish between essence and existence as constituents of being. Their philosophy is not concerned with demonstrating that God actually exists. Rather, their philosophy is concerned with showing how God, as reality, is present to human experience. Their concern is the presence and reality of God. Their conception of God is not the God of Greek metaphysics. The philosophy of Marcel and Berdyaev is an integrally Christian philosophy whose God is wholly and exclusively the God of my developing Christian theism.

The Phenomenological Development of my Christian Theism

In the development of my Christian theism God's existence is a matter of experiential fact and, not of necessity. That is, to exist necessarily and, to be present experientially are quite different understandings. God, as reality beyond the totality of being, as I understand, it is revealed not out of necessity but out of love. An emergent motivation, on God's part, not an external cause, is the operative motive revealing God's love to me. There is then, beyond the totality of all existing things, a presence present to me through my experience. When some other presence makes itself felt and makes me to be more than I would be were I not exposed to its influence, my belief has true foundation. To express this foundation requires an adequate philosophy, which in turn gives rise to an adequate theology. What needs to be proven to me is not that God objectively exists. Rather, what requires a demonstration for me, then, since it is not immediately obvious, is God's presence to me. As a believer, as a philosopher and theologian, whether, and in what sense, in what way, and with what consequences, God is present to me is to be determined philosophically and subsequently expressed theologically.

Philosophically, my human way of being, my self and my personality are constituted by my consciousness, which uniquely signifies myself to me. Thus, for me to be a subject, that is a person, is to be an object to myself. I no longer understand my personality in relation to an external nature. In other words, my personality is a manifestation of my self, at a certain stage in its evolution. Consciousness and the interpretation of experience constitute my personality, which is the equivalent of my life and existence. As a person, I am a being who desires to evolve beyond my present self. However, if I as a Christian look at the world and understand nature through Hellenic eyes, I will find it necessary to look to the past and not beyond myself and subsequently assert the power of God over me. In Hellenist eyes I remain a creature with no opportunity to evolve to a co-creator status. Greek philosophy introduced a spilt into the ontological relationship of God and humanity and caused a metaphysical dualism. However, phenomenologically understood, the God beyond me does not have absolute power in the classical sense over me. Let me say, however, that nature does have its own natural causes effective independently of God's purposes. The fundamental relation between God and me consists, not in a hierarchical relationship of power, but in the mutual presence of God and me in a conscious unity within creation wherein I become a co-creator. As I dehellenize my Christian theism my faith is recast and the meaning of religion is expressed in terms that do not imply God's absolute power over me, nor my inordinate submission to God.

In recent times, as Western philosophy has diverged more and more from its Greek foundations the concept of the supernatural has lost its usefulness for my Christian theism. This is so since the mainstream of Catholic philosophy has remained Scholastic and therefore, somewhat unsympathetic to the contemporary scientific understanding of human nature. Thus, Catholic theology, especially the school of thought that has abandoned Scholasticism increasingly seeks non-Christian, secular thought for support. This is the case also for the Teilhardians, that is, those philosophers committed to the views of Teilhard de Chardin

(1881–1955) or those other thinkers whose philosophical or specialized disciplines were never dominated by scholasticism, disciplines such as, scriptural studies.

Concerning my worship of God it might be better understood to be a rendering of myself present to the presence of God. I may render myself present to God in interior prayer, which sends no message to God, yet through which I receive God's presence. This interior prayer is grace. As well, I may worship in public ceremonies, which visibly and audibly unite my worship with others through a collective presence within the presence of the present God. In this context of worship the concept of the supernatural is not a necessary part of my belief, if I conceive the founder of Christianity as Albert Nolan (1978) suggests.[5] However, what is absolutely fundamental to my belief is the Spirit of God, which is perceived in the Christian doctrine of grace. As immanent in me, the Spirit of God is known as the gift (*donum*) of God. However, the traditional view of grace continues to be understood as grace building upon nature. In the immanent philosophical view, which is a phenomenological understanding, nature ceases to be juxtaposed to grace. Rather, nature reveals grace because that is how nature has been created. Nature is essentially contingent upon grace and I derive my nature, as it were, from being existentially, not metaphysically, related to grace. Thus, grace, as God's gift, is God's presence to me.

Contemporary theologians, both Eastern and Western, are beginning to realize that the structure of church government, which reflects

---

5 In the Introduction to *Jesus before Christianity*, he writes: "The primary purpose of this book is neither faith nor history. It can be read and is designed to be read without faith. Nothing about Jesus will be presupposed or assumed. The reader is invited to take a serious and honest look at a man who lived in first-century Palestine and to try to see him through the eyes of his contemporaries. My interest is in the man as he was before he became the object of Christian faith."

traditional, classical theism, must change. Alexander Bogolepov (1963) has accurately noted that for practical considerations, ecclesiastical districts were established from the very beginning of the Christian era in conformity with the political division of the state and, under the Roman Empire, the Christian assembly became a state church. The present political governing apparatus, based on territorial notions and not on God's grace or divine charism is an impediment to the ecclesial governance of the church for the future. Such territorial notions often do not conform to our lived, that is, existential social conditions. Nor do they reflect God's presence or charism. Further, it would be a theological error for theologians to promote the idea of a universal territorial superchurch composed of all the faithful based merely on the philosophical notions of human political expediency. In this connection we must remember that a universal humanism does not exist, but that individual humans do. Further, our humanity, as a phenomenological notion, is expressed through a variety of individual philosophical, political and cultural patterns to which God is present.

In modern times, phenomenological, or continental philosophy, has slowly been replacing classical philosophy as the underpinning philosophy in much civilized human development. The Church is one organization of civilized human development where this is occurring. As well, various other of civilized human organizations, such as governmental, financial and societal structures, are entering into dialogue with each other on an international scale. A phenomenological philosophical interpretation does not describe the same phenomenon that a classical philosophical explanation does. The former includes my consciousness where the latter does not necessarily include it, which accounts for a different phenomenon being recognized. Further, phenomenological philosophers and theologians in their interpretations do not abandon their ideological origins and seek new perspectives, without a focus, to replace them. Rather, they engage their specific cultures and demographic traditions to create a new meaningful philosophical understanding. This new understanding comes from their reflective experience, which arises out of their ideological origins. In contrast to this approach some contemporary philosophers and theologians, both Eastern and Western, seem to prefer a return to a perceived golden era in scholastic philosophical and theological thinking rather than create new meaningful understandings from their experience. Falling into this temptation, some Latin theologians are abandoning the phenomenological orientation introduced by Vatican II. In a similar manner some Orthodox theologians suffer from the same nostalgic desire for a perceived philosophical golden age with respect to their ecclesiastical traditions.

It sometimes happens that particular local communities, which are culturally identifiable and unified with respect to their ecclesiologies, present themselves as universally valid models for all Christ's faithful. This approach will fail in practice because any universal identity of the faithful cannot be that of a particular community. In fact, the faithful are cultureless as a universal identity. In short, there is no universal culture. Rather, individual communities of the faithful are uniquely identifiable as a culture within a culture. To make the case further, I suggest that there are as many personal identities as there are cultural communities. Writing from a political perspective, Victor Segesvary (2003) lists particular identities that one may possess within a given culture. They are; being a member of a cult, football club, or a literary circle. Within the community, an individual may embrace all or only a few such identities. However, Segesvary notes that an irresolvable problem comes to the fore only when one of the identities is a fundamentalist one and is linked to an ethnic group or nation, a religion, or a cultural community. Thus, according to his thinking, if my ecclesial cultural identity is narrowly fundamentalist it presents an irresolvable problem with respect to the development of my Christian theism.

Phenomenological philosophers and theologians do not accept that the Church can integrate the faithful by force with reference to their belief. The Church attempted this, however, during the Spanish Inquisition when scholasticism dominated the Western Church's thinking. Nor can any universal Church government, through propaganda, create a religious identity among the faithful as a unified community. Rather, true religious identity is achieved through the faithful participating in the decisions about their own affairs in the local parochial and cultural context. This religious identity achieved through participating in decisions would require a corresponding reduction in universal legislation governing the faithful. Ecclesiastical government, in contrast to ecclesial governance, is a hierarchical bureaucracy and a totally impersonal way of determining and managing the affairs of the faithful. And, the current crisis in ecclesiastical government is of the type that characterizes all contemporary bureaucratically organized bodies. Accordingly, all things being considered and because I am one of the faithful, this bureaucratic crisis affects the development of my Christian theism.

In late Modernity, rapid technological advances have increased the opportunities for bureaucratic control over the faithful who live in a secular and Westernized culture. The Internet is a case in point. With the advent of the Internet a new ideology, not merely technology, is in the process of being developed with the assistance of scientific advancement. Regretfully, at this point, it often seems to be a negative ideology, potentially threatening the person, in that the Internet is a de-personalizing forum since there is no need for physical, that is, embodied contact among the users of the Internet. For an insightful treatment of this development see Paul Doyle's (2006), *Analog People in a Digital World*. In the internet virtual community there is no possibility of a humanitarian incarnation such as constitutes existential physical human relationships. Virtual reality is the simulated computerized version of existence, which presents many philosophical and theological challenges to our incarnated humanity. To my mind, a non-incarnated and technological, that is, virtual experience cannot reflect any true human society or community since the simulation by the virtual decision-makers is not identical to the lived experience of actual persons. The inordinate and uncritical use of internet technology by an individual is likely to create eventually incompetent, that is, non-humanized, non-incarnated, individuals. However, on balance, the internet has been known to stimulate the human mind to develop its knowledge, whereas television, the other modern medium, has been known to dull the mind's activity. In short, the internet turns my mind on and television turns my mind off.

Notwithstanding this observation, however, a lack of competent incarnated and humanized individuals, or personnel formed merely within the virtual reality of the ideology of the Internet, subsequently creates a lack of competence within the Church's theological teaching authority, the Magisterium. As non-humanized and non-incarnated individuals, as it were, the understanding of Christian theism will be affected accordingly. It is for this reason, then, that any ambition on my part as a philosopher and theologian for government of a universal church, brought about solely by a virtual and technological means, is abandoned as unrealistic. And, dare I say it such virtual technology should be also abandoned as non-human? Victor Segesvary (2003) reminds us that humanity, as a community, is too big an entity to be the bearer of a single shared culture. Yet individual cultures do require a community as their bearer. In this respect, our contemporary cultural world is not different from the ancient cultural worlds. Although many contemporary philosophers and theologians do suggest that Modernity is different from everything that has preceded it and that modern humanity, the result of an evolutionary process, is an exceptional gift to the universe. As Henri Bergson (1944) has summarized it, for these reasons it would be wrong to regard humanity, such as we have it, before our eyes, as pre- figured in the evolutionary movement.

There are a variety of ideologies identified by philosophers and theologians. Ethnic, religious, cultural and linguistic traditions may become transnational ideologies. True, one culture can adopt the traditions of another. In a religious context there will be conflicts, of necessity, among groups of the faithful, that is, parishes and local churches, which confess a particular ideology. When cultural variety is ignored, as is the case occasionally in our historical, political and religious context, an expectation about a future global union of churches, patterned after a world civil government, seems logical to some philosophers and theologians. Such civil and universal expectation, however, has a negative affect on the development of my Christian theistic theology. Note that I say a global union, not unity, of churches. In our present circumstances, were this global union of churches to come about the governmental apparatus of the churches would no doubt resemble the dominant secular culture of the West. The problem in accepting the Western cultural pattern for government in the Churches, as I understand it, is that Western secular education, being technologically driven, has given me a specialized knowledge about the world that is not conducive to the development of my contemporary Christian theism. This specialized knowledge lacks an encompassing view of the world. Bits of information from contemporary science and technology can only become appropriate knowledge after an individual mentally processes them to produce a coherent whole, or a holistic unity.

Phenomenologically understood, this holistic unity is greater than the sum of its individual parts. In Henri Bergson's (1944), words: To form an idea of the whole of life cannot consist in combining simple ideas that have been left behind in us by life itself in the course of its evolution. In short, contemporary science and technology have only re-packaged scholasticism, but they have not introduced a holistic unity, in the process. Further, since individual bits of information do not constitute a holistic unity, a world union of churches would lack the shared beliefs, values, symbols, language, history and customs that would constitute a holistic community of churches.

A universal governing ideology cannot be constructed phenomenologically. Phenomenologically, an understanding of others, their civilizations, and ways of life is to be discerned through dialogue and the examination of relationships without the interference of preconceived ideas and without the presumed superiority of the Western scholastic philosophical and theological tradition. Our common humanity suggests to many philosophical and theological thinkers the need of a universal humanitarian understanding to designate human beings. Victor Segesvary (2003) notes that universalism is a millennia-old dream of humanity dating from the time of the Stoics. The desire for universalism was evident also in the medieval Church and is reflected in modern ideologies like Marxism and liberalism. It should be remembered, however, that universalism does not denote universality. Universalism is a scholastic philosophical term, whereas universality is a phenomenological philosophical term. Thus, normative universalism is an ideology, which reflects the particular moral and ethical principles arising within a culture. It is highly doubtful that a universal moral and ethical principle applicable to all peoples and in all times can be drawn from a specific civilization. To attempt this would be a philosophical, as well as political, mistake. Were this to occur, however, normative universalism would be a misnomer, as well as, a deficient state of affairs comprised of nothing but a local community's mores. In contrast, given my intent to develop a proper future for ecclesial governance and a proper future for the development of Christian theism what I must understand is a humanitarian universality that is holistically discerned and based on common human and social origin.

The foregoing discussion, as laid out in the previous chapters, prompts me to the following conclusions with respect to theological reconstruction and the phenomenological development of my Christian theism. In the present status quo, the government of the Church, both Eastern and Western must move from a classical ecclesiastical methodology (an architectural methodology) to a phenomenological ecclesial methodology (an organic methodology) in constructing its governing apparatus. This will enable a proper and appropriate development of theism by the Christian faithful of our times. The main obstacles to organic ecclesial governance are the various architecturally constructed civic ideologies and authorities that determine modern individualistic cultures. The uncritical acceptance of these civil ideologies and authorities impede a proper development of Christian theism. By way of further example, territorialism, not territoriality, is the product of an architecturally constructed civic ideology with its roots in classical Hellenistic philosophy. By way of contrast, territoriality has its roots in phenomenological philosophy. The same observation may be made for the notions of Catholicism and Catholicity, nationalism and nationality, historicism and historicity, humanism and humanity, communism and community, etc. as noted above. The understanding of territoriality as describing a community encompasses a notion, which includes more than the community's mere physical location. It embraces the linguistic, cultural and historical understandings of a community. A phenomenological methodology explains this shift from "-ism" to "-ity" in philosophical thinking. In adopting a phenomenological methodology, with respect to governance, dioceses in the future cannot be determined by territorialism, but must be constituted territorially. That is, they will be constituted through an experience of residence, which embraces the affects of linguistic, cultural and historical understandings in a given physical space upon the earth. The experience of residence in this physical space will constitute a diocesan framework of organic governance, replacing the inherited architectural government that presently exists. Dioceses that are constituted out of an experiential cultural framework, or organic governance and, are not dependent on physical or political territory, will be directed by governors who lay claim to a limited, or contextual sovereignty, based on their existential interpretation of experience. Nor will organically governed dioceses be bound by a theoretical or political acceptance of civil territory. Thus, my understanding of Christian theism generated in this context will be constituted within a phenomenological, not classical approach.

Within the Church of the future, I suspect that multilateralism will not remain a normative principle. When this happens, the question will arise: could our present cultural ecclesial communities lose their role if they are not embedded territorially? I suggest that the answer is, no. Multilateral communities will be constituted non-spatially and non-territorially, that is, they will be recognized phenomenologically and designated by another term than multilateral. Such phenomenologically recognized communities will be constituted by humanitarian communicative relationships, which depend, unlike the Internet, on embodied relationships. The development of non-multilateral communities suggests to me that the cultural problems of religion, language, education, administration, etc., can be resolved within an ecclesial community that eliminates the idea of national sovereignty. I suggest that in a new order of organic church governance, the notions of co-ordination and cooperation will replace a sovereign and centralized ideology, which will no longer be useful. This is so, since the ecclesial principle of subsidiarity locates the power of the decision-making process in the hands of those affected by the decision-making process. In contrast, sovereign and centralized bureaucracies take power away from those affected by the decision-making process. To act locally and link up globally demonstrate the dynamic of an organic, non-territorial ecclesial order, that is, an order of governance, not government. Whether or not such governance is workable in all societies is an open question. However, such governance seems more in keeping with my Christian notion of God's kingdom that is not limited by physical territory.

It is likely that in the future there will be no universal canon law, but only regional particular canon laws. In a phenomenologically constituted community the constitution of canon law will be a self-regulating exercise as the law emerges from both public and private experience through the various interpretations undertaken by the faithful. In future Canon Law there will be no penal sanctions but rather suggestions for remedial action. That is to say, the constitution of canon law will be such that laws will not be in external conflict with one another but, rather, be corrective of innate personal and corporate behaviour. This suggestion is consonant with modern experience in that there is an equality of opportunity, but not necessarily an equality of outcome. To suggest remedial action for personal and corporate behaviour is characteristic of the God of my Christian theism.

In this book I proposed that a phenomenologically understood ecclesial community reflects a new ecclesiology that is based upon knowledge of our collective experience, and not on the mere notion of territorialism. The option of governance I advocate for the future, in contrast to the present traditional architectural structure, calls for a new organic ecclesiology, not territorially re-ordered but phenomenologically reconstituted. This re-constitution calls for, on a continual basis, a re-appraisal of the development of my Christian theistic theology.

References

Berdyaev, Nicolas. 1957. *The Beginning and the End*. New York: Harper.

Bergson, Henri. 1944. *Creative Evolution*. New York: Modern Library.

Bogolepov, Alexander. 1963. *Toward an American Orthodox Church: The Establishment of an Autocephalous Orthodox Church*. New York: Morehouse-Barlow.

Canadian Conference of Catholic Bishops. 2009. *Ordo: Liturgical Calendar*. Ottawa: CCCB Publications.

Demant. V. A. 1947. *Our Culture: Its Roots and Present Crisis*. London: SPCK.

Dewart, Leslie. 1966. *The Future of Belief: Theism in a World Come of Age*. New York: Herder & Herder.

———. 1989. *Evolution and Consciousness: The Role of Speech in the Origin and Development of Human Nature*. Toronto: University of Toronto Press.

Dillenberger, John. 1969. *Contours of Faith: Changing Forms of Christian Thought*. New York: Abingdon.

Domenach, Jean-Marie, and Robert de Montvalon. 1967. *The Catholic Avant-Garde: French Catholicism Since World War II*. New York: Holt, Rinehart & Winston.

Doyle, Paul. 2006. *Analog People in a Digital World*. Winnipeg, MB: ArtBookbindery.com.

Earle, William, and James Edie and John Wild. 1963. *Christianity and Existentialism*. Evanston, IL: Northwestern University Press.

Fawkes, Alfred. 1913. *Studies in Modernism*. London: Smith and Elder.

Flannery, Austin. 1996. *The Basic Sixteen Documents of Vatican Council II: Constitutions and Decrees*. New York: Costello.

Garbett, Cyril. 1947. *The Claims of the Church of England*. London: Hodder & Stoughton.

Gardner, Percy. 1926. *Modernism in the English Church*. London: Methuen.

Gilkey, Langdon. 1975. *Catholicism Confronts Modernity: A Protestant View*. New York: Crossroad.

———. 1985. "The Role of the Theologian in Contemporary Society," in *The Thought of Paul Tillich*, ed. James Luther Adams, Wilhelm Pauck and Roger Lincoln Shinn, 330-83. San Francisco: Harper.

Gilson, Etienne. 1968. "On Behalf of the Handmaid," in *Renewal of Religious Thought*, ed.   L. K. Shook, 236 - 49. Montréal, PQ: Palm Publishers.

Habermas, Jürgen. 1992. *The Philosophical Discourse of Modernity: Twelve Lectures.* Cambridge, MA: MIT Press.

Harry Girvetz, et al. 1966. *Science, Folklore and Philosophy.* New York: Harper and Row.

Hinners, R. C. 1967. "The Challenge of De-hellenization," in *The Future of Belief Debate*, ed. Gregory Baum, 197- 208. New York: Herder & Herder.

Hughes, Philip. 1947. *A Popular History of the Catholic Church.* London: Burns and Oates.

John Paul II. 1993. *Veritas Splendor.* Ottawa: CCCB.

John Paul II. 1994. *Crossing the Threshold of Hope.* New York: Alfred Knopf.

Kaucha, Krzysztof. 2009. "Contemporary Theology in the Service of Person and Culture in Europe," in *Theologie im Osten Europas Europas seit 1989.* (Theologie Ost-West, Band 12) Berlin: LIT.

King, Henry Church.1901. *Reconstruction in Theology.* New York: Macmillan.

Kobler, John. 2000. "Vatican II Theology Needs Philosophy," *The Modern Schoolman*, 73: 89-95.

Koestenbaum, P. 1967. "Religion in the Tradition of Phenomenology," in *Religion in Philosophical and Cultural Perspective: A New Approach to the Philosophy of Religion Through Cross-disciplinary Studies,* ed. J. Clayton Feaver and William Horosz, 174-214. Princeton, New Jersey: D Van Nostrand.

Laycock, Stephen William and James Hart. 1986. *Essays in Phenomenological Theology*. New York: State University of New York Press.

Liderbach, Daniel. 2001. "Modernism in the Roman Church." *Explorations: Journal for Adventurous Thought*. 20: 17-36.

Lilley, Leslie. 1909. *The Programme of Modernism: A Reply to the Encyclical of Pius X, Pascendi Dominici Gregis*. London: Fisher Unwin.

Luijpen, William. 1966. *Phenomenology and Humanism: A Primer in Existential Phenomenology*. Pittsburgh, PA: Duquesne University Press.

Lurie, Yuval. 2000. *Cultural Beings: Reading the Philosophers of Genesis*. Amsterdam, NL: Rodopi.

Macquarrie, John. 1975. *Thinking about God*. New York: Harper & Row.

Maxwell, P. 1986. "Some Reflections on the So-called Phenomenological Method in the Study of Religion." *Religion in Southern Africa* 7: 15-25.

Moran, Dermont. 2005. *Edmund Husserl: Founder of Phenomenology*. Cambridge Malden, MA: Polity Press.

Moreall, J. 1983. "Can Theological Language Have Hidden Meaning?" *Religious Studies* 19: 43-56.

Murray, Michael. 1975. *Modern Critical Theory: A Phenomenological Introduction.* The Hague: Nijhoff.

Nolan, Albert. 1978. *Jesus before Christianity.* Maryknoll, N.Y.: Orbis Books.

Ott, H. 1967. "Language and Understanding," in *New Theology* 4, ed. M. E. Marty and D. G. Peerman, 124-46. New York: Macmillan.

Petre, Maude. 1912. *Autobiography and Life of George Tyrrell.* (Two volumes). London: Arnold.

Raschke, C. 1979. *The Alchemy of the Word: Language and the End of Theology.* Atlanta: American Academy of Religion, Studies in Religion.

Reardon, Bernard. 1970. *Roman Catholic Modernism.* London: Adams & Charles Black.

Ryba, Thomas. 1991. *The Essence of Phenomenology and its Meaning for the Scientific Study of Religion.* New York: Peter Lang.

Sabatier, Auguste. 2003 [1904?]. *Religions of Authority and the Religion of the Spirit.* Whitefish, MT: Kessinger Publishing Reprint.

Sagovsky, Nicholas. 1990. *On God's Side: A Life of George Tyrrell.* Oxford: Clarendon Press.

Segesvary, Victor. 2003. *World State, Nation States, or Non-Centralized Institutions? A Vision of the Future in Politics*. Lanham, MD: University Press of America.

Tymieniecka, Anna T. 1962. *Phenomenology and Science in Contemporary European Thought*. New York: Noonday.

Tyrrell, George. 1906. *Lex Credendi: A Sequal to Lex Orandi*. London: Longmans.

———. 1907. *Oil and Wine*. London: Longmans.

———. 1907. *Through Scylla and Charybdis, or the Old Theology and the New*. London: Longmans, Green.

———. 1910. *The Church and the Future*. London: Priory Press.

van de Pol, W. H. 1952. *The Christian Dilemma: Catholic Church — Reformation*. London: Dent.

van Rensburg, Johan Janse. 2007. "Seminar on Research Methodology." North-West University, Potchefstroom Campus, South Africa, August 30-31.

von Hügel, Friedrich. 1912. *Eternal Life: A Study of Its Implications and Applications*. Edinburgh: T & T Clark.

Waardenburg, J. D. 1973. "Research on Meaning in Religion," in *Religion, Culture and Methodology*, ed. Th. P. Van Baaren and H. J. W. Drijvers, 109-36. The Hague: Mouton.

Wolf, Donald. 1966. *Current Trends in Theology*, ed. Donald Wolf and
James Schall. New York: Image Doubleday.

Zuurdeeg, W. F. 1960. "The Nature of Theological Language." *Journal
of Religion* 40: 1-8.

About the Contributors

Allan Savage, ordained in 1978, is Director of the Adult Faith Office of the Roman Catholic Diocese of Thunder Bay, Canada. After obtaining his doctorate in theology he authored various books on philosophical, theological and spiritual topics. A former Sessional Lecturer in the in the Faculty of Theology, University of Winnipeg, he is presently pastor of St Patrick's Parish, Québec City, QC, Canada.

James Bishop, a life-long learner, lives in Thunder Bay, Ontario, Canada. He holds degrees in Education and Theology and has teaching experience in Canada and the United States. He is married and having raised a family, which is his main interest, he remains active in his parish while he contemplates a writing career.

By Same Author

A Phenomenological Understanding of Certain Liturgical Texts. The Anglican Collects for Advent and the Roman Catholic Collects for Lent. 2001, University Press of America.

> This book examines the philosophical premises underlying the language used in liturgical prayers. Scholastic philosophy, the dominant philosophical perspective in the West, is no longer satisfactory for contemporary religious formulation. Phenomenological philosophy appears to be replacing scholastic philosophy in forming and understanding personal and communal religious beliefs. The Collects of the Anglican and Roman Catholic Eucharistic liturgies for Advent and Lent were examined, re-written and "field tested." The focus group for the field testing was composed of individuals who formally engage in research into spirituality and religious experiences. A Phenomenological Understanding of Certain Liturgical Texts encourages further investigation into the growing use of phenomenology in liturgical understanding based on a discernible trend in this direction.

Faith, Hope and Charity as Character Traits in Adler's Individual Psychology. With Related Essays in Spirituality and Phenomenology. 2003, University Press of America.

> In Part One, Sheldon Nicholl offers an outline of Adler's life and the basics of his Individual Psychology. Allan Savage examines the relationship between Individual Psychology and Pastoral Theology. Special attention is given to the role

of cognitive therapy. The cardinal virtues of faith, hope and charity are explored, in some detail, in the context of Adler's Individual Psychology. As character traits they are found to be in accord with the development of Adler's notion ofGemeinschaftsgefühl. Part Two is a compilation of previously published essays in American and British journals. One section consists of a set of six exchanges between Erik Mansager and Allan Savage over the concept of "critical collaboration." Other previously published essays by Savage incorporate Adlerian themes. However, chapter eight is not specifically Adlerian in content. Since the root of Adler's Individual Psychology is anchored in German philosophical thought of the early 1900's this chapter explores notions derived from the later Heidegger and the thought of Husserl.

A Contemporary Understanding of Religious Belief Within Mental Health. 2007, Melrose Books.

This short book suggests the need for psychiatrists to work with the knowledge of theology so that mentally ill patients who hold strong religious beliefs may receive appropriate treatment. The work is introduced by discussing the definition of mental illness, the meaning of religious belief in modern society and the view that psychiatry has of it. He states that "Theology can make a significant contribution to the integration of mental health and religious belief." Reverend Savage promotes the phenomenological approach to understanding religious belief, an approach that concentrates on the study of consciousness and the objects of direct experience. He claims that secularisation in modern society has caused "...a fracture between religion and spirituality." He then discusses how society influences the form that religious belief takes and how it decides what is or what is not "normal." The author explains how psychiatry today is a combination of psychoanalysis and the chemical management of neurological processes. It is debatable whether general practitioners should prescribe antidepressants without prior consultation with a psychiatrist. The role of the psychiatrist seems to be diminishing, but "there is no question that for the near future the psychiatrist will remain a moral agent on behalf of the community;" a position that was traditionally held by priests. Reverend Savage writes in a very learned style and his book may be a useful addition to the bookshelves of undergraduate and practising psychiatrists.

The Ecology: A 'New to You" View - An Orthodox Theological Ecology. 2008, www.artbookbindery.com.

The ideas presented in this book, in fact, are not new. They represent problems arising from the new orientation of the Western World that followed the Great War of 1914-1918. Much contemporary theology still deals with issues that have been identified as "Modernism" by the ecclesiastical authorities of an earlier day. What is new in this book, however, is a phenomenological theological interpretation in the context of a contemporary global ecology, and not in the context of the traditional ecclesiastical politics of Eastern and Western Churches.

Dehellenization and Dr Dewart Revisited: A First Person Philosophical Reflection. 2009, www.createspace.com.

I have written this book as a serious first person reflection on a philosophical topic. I have not made a systematic presentation of ideas or exposé of a body of thought or presented a collection of philosophical ideas. Rather, the book is a brief account of my personal thinking, on the topic of dehellenization, as I remember it, through reading the works of other religious philosophers. Among all the disciplines available to assist theologians in the critical task of collaborative reflection, a scientific philosophy is a most fundamental one. Psychology, sociology, history, anthropology, etc., make a contribution to the task. However, it is only philosophy that is in a uniquely privileged position to undertake the task of theological reflection. This is so since the act of philosophizing upon one's experience is universal in the sense that it constitutes human reflection, whereas other disciplines merely augment human reflection.

Philosophical Memoires: Constructing Christian Theology in the Contemporary World. 2009, www.createspace.com.

In this book I discuss the philosophical construction of Christian theology from a subjective point of view. I follow an existential approach and rely on my experience to give direction to my thought. Drawing on insights from Leslie Dewart, I recast the ideas and notions inherited from the Hellenist philosophical tradition and present two "case studies" that illustrate the role of a dehellenized philosophy in the construction of contemporary Christian theology. These two case studies, the first "dehellenization" and the second, "Orthodox Canon Law," are deliberately poles apart to show that phenomenal theological interpretation, which transcends the conditions of time and culture assists in solving these contemporary theological problems.